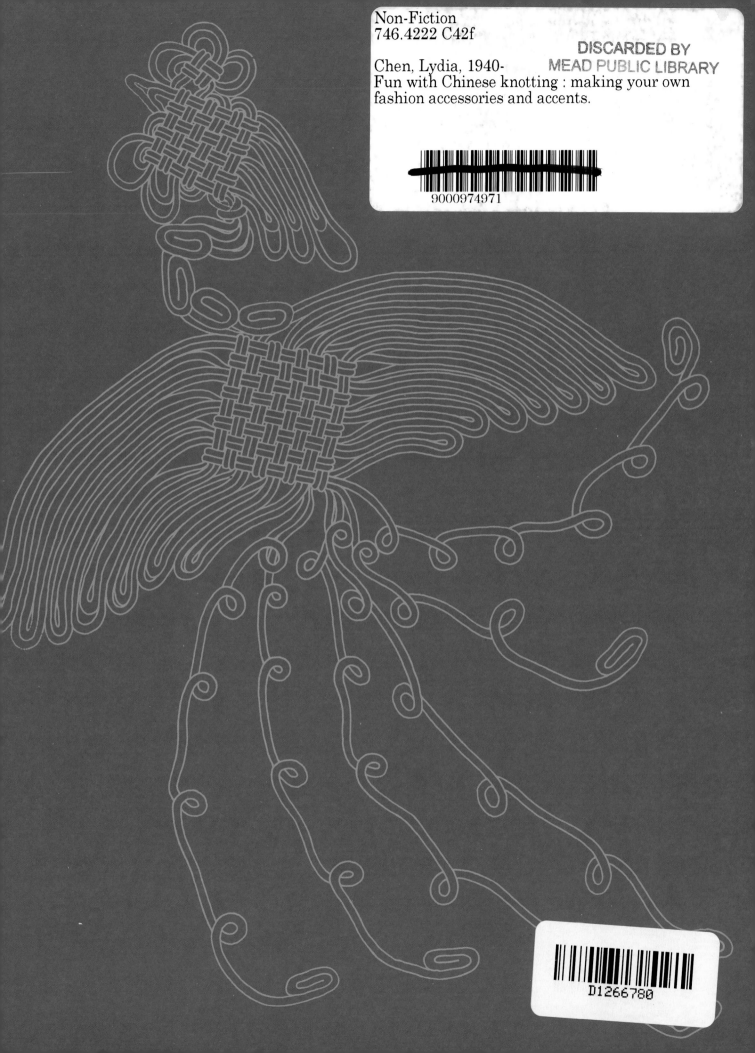

Fun with Chinese Knotting

Making Your Own Fashion Accessories and Accents

by Lydia Chen

TUTTLE PUBLISHING
Tokyo • Rutland, Vermont • Singapore

Published by Tuttle Publishing, an imprint of Periplus Editions (HK) Ltd, with editorial offices at 354 Innovation Drive, North Clarendon, Vermont 05759, USA, and 130 Joo Seng Road #06-01, Singapore 368357.

Library of Congress Control Number 2006933108
ISBN 0 8048 3678 7

Distributed by

North America, Latin America and Europe
Tuttle Publishing
364 Innovation Drive
North Clarendon, VT 05759, USA
Tel: 1 (802) 773 8930;
Fax: 1 (802) 773 6993
info@tuttlepublishing.com
www.tuttlepublishing.com

Japan
Tuttle Publishing
Yaekari Building, 3rd Floor
5-4-12 Osaki, Shinagawa-ku
Tokyo 141-0032
Tel: (81) 5437 0171
Fax: (81) 5437 0755
tuttle-sales@gol.com

Asia Pacific
Berkeley Books Pte Ltd
130 Joo Seng Road #06-01
Singapore 368357
Tel: (65) 6280 1330;
Fax: (65) 6280 6290
inquiries@periplus.com.sg
www.periplus.com

First edition
10 09 08 07 06   10 9 8 7 6 5 4 3 2 1

Printed in Singapore

TUTTLE PUBLISHING® is a registered trademark of Tuttle Publishing, a division of Periplus Editions (HK) Ltd.

Contents

The Resurgence of Chinese Knotting

Chinese knotting, sometimes referred to as Chinese macramé, is a craft that is increasingly gaining popularity in both the East and the West as more and more people come to realize the benefits of traditional handwork in a frenetic world of urban industrialization, mass production, modern transportation and computer technology. This traditional craft provides not only a wonderful means of relaxation but also allows the artistic satisfaction of producing a personalized work of art, especially on clothing and objects and in home décor. Asian fashion designers often add the finishing touches to their work with knots, while homemakers add elegance to their houses with this fine art. Nowadays, handcraft traders in the East send huge quantities of Chinese knots overseas, while specialty shops selling ornamental Chinese knots have mushroomed in both the East and the West.

Chinese knotting, literally "the joining of two cords," is an ancient and revered art form in China and an integral part of Chinese life. Since ancient times, Chinese knots have been fashioned from cotton and silk for a variety of practical and decorative purposes: to record events, aid in fishing and hunting, wrap and tie items, embellish personal attire, ornament other works of art such as ancient portraits, and communicate. Knots in the form of tassels were used to enhance the appearance of chopsticks, fans, scepters, talismans and even spectacle cases in the later Ching Dynasty. The earliest recorded use of decorative knots is on bronze vessels dating to the Warring States Period (700 BC). Chinese knots have decorated both the fixtures of palace halls and the daily implements of country folk. They have also appeared in paintings, sculptures and folk art. In Chinese poetry, knots symbolize the emotional ties of lovers, and ornamental knots are traditional keepsakes exchanged by lovers.

In China up until the late 1930s, decorative knotting was a widely practiced pastime in both rural and urban areas. On festive occasions and during important rites of passage such as weddings, intricate and beautiful knots, tied by family and friends, were visible everywhere, lending both a festive and personal air to important occasions. The knots were an aesthetic expression of Chinese folk symbolism, expressing wishes for good fortune and wealth or the joys of love and marriage. From the 1930s up until the late 1970s, when the art of macramé became popular in the West – causing a simultaneous revival of interest in Chinese knotting – traditional knotting was barely seen except in museums where examples were shown as relics of an ancient culture or in antique shops where they were greedily snapped up by foreign buyers intrigued by the intricate craftsmanship and magnificent color combinations of the exquisitely symmetrical knots on sale. Today, the art of knotting has attracted worldwide attention, achieving breakthroughs in both design and application.

This second book by Lydia Chen, a well-known and highly respected authority on Chinese knotting and a pioneer in the revival of the craft, builds on her first one, *Chinese Knotting: Creative Designs That Are Easy and Fun!* (Tuttle, 2003) and opens up a brand new world of Chinese knotting applications. In this book, the author focuses on the use of Chinese knots as fashion accessories – hair ornaments, earrings, necklaces, pendants, brooches, belts, bracelets and rings – and as accents on clothing, as well as accessories on other objects, in the hope that readers will be encouraged to revolutionize the art form by developing their own styles. The author builds on the basic knots by introducing more complex examples – combinations and variations of the simple knots – and also teaches readers

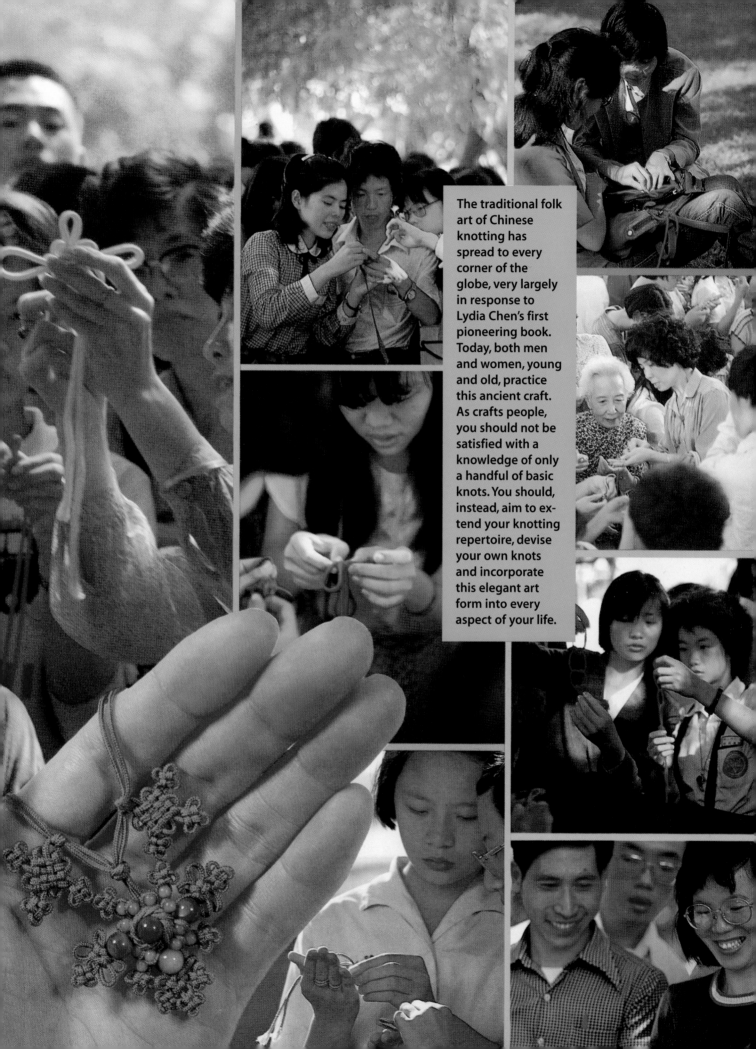

The traditional folk art of Chinese knotting has spread to every corner of the globe, very largely in response to Lydia Chen's first pioneering book. Today, both men and women, young and old, practice this ancient craft. As crafts people, you should not be satisfied with a knowledge of only a handful of basic knots. You should, instead, aim to extend your knotting repertoire, devise your own knots and incorporate this elegant art form into every aspect of your life.

how to make tassels. Moreover, the repertoire of materials has been extended – from silk and cotton cords to those made of leather, cloth, plastic, metal, paper and clay – thereby stimulating further creativity and innovation.

This practical manual starts by recapping the basic principles and skills required to tie knots, as well as the materials that can be used, and gives handy tips on knot formation and color blending. Full color photographs in the second part of the book illustrate how knot formations can be applied to clothing and

Design and make your o

other objects used in everyday life. The next two parts – the technical sections – present clear two-color, step-by-step instructions for making nine of the most basic knots in the Chinese knotting repertoire, nineteen compound knots created by the author from the basic knots and, for the first time, five tassels. The last part of the book presents sketches and step-by-step instructions for making the 135 knot formations illustrated in full color throughout the book. Once the knots have been mastered, the sky is the limit for the creative and dedicated knotter.

Just as each person has his or her own personality, each Chinese knot has its own unique beauty and character. Here, ten charming girls display with pride and joy some of the knot formations taught in this book as fashion accessories and accents on clothing: belts, pendants, and decorations on hats and bags.

...inese knots. Charm everyone you meet.

Let your imagination run wild in the world of Chinese knots. A vast variety of materials can be used, either singly or in combination, to make single knots as well as more complex knot formations. The lucky knot shown here is made of metal cords and its loops embellished with love beans. It will make an ideal gift for your partner. The graceful butterfly knot below it is made from plastic cords, a modern and trendy material which will appeal to the younger set.

Designing Chinese Knots

Chinese knots (and tassels) have traditionally been used to decorate accessories and artifacts such as jade, fans, wind chimes and lanterns. Tied by family or friends, they have also long been used as colorful hangings on festive occasions or during important rites of passage such as weddings. The knots themselves were never considered to have much artistic value and little attention was paid to how they were made. They were simply there and taken for granted!

Yet, when we look closely at Chinese knots, we find that each is an extremely systematic, intricate and delicate item, the fine details reflecting the very thoughts, feelings and artistry of the ancient Chinese women who made them. Only then do we see that knotting is an art in itself.

Once we acknowledge the artistic merit of knots, we can break away from the concept of a knot being merely an accessory to enhance the elegance of some other, main object. We can make it the main focus of attention and embellish it with other ornaments. In this way, the design of Chinese knots offers infinite creative possibilities.

But to design a simple or compound knot and to explore its potential, one must first of all have a sound knowledge of the basic skills of knotting. One also needs to have a knowledge of such fundamentals as the choice of format, the most suitable colors, the most appropriate cord materials and the best embellishments. This chapter provides the basic skills necessary to help readers design and apply their own knots and also gives handy tips on knotting.

Introduce elements from modern art into Chinese knotting. Here, multiple colored cords add fresh appeal to the inherent beauty of traditional forms, injecting a new dimension into the art. Colors outside the normal spectrum – gold, silver, black and white – used in combination with the basic seven colors can produce dazzling results.

前言

《如何設計中國結》

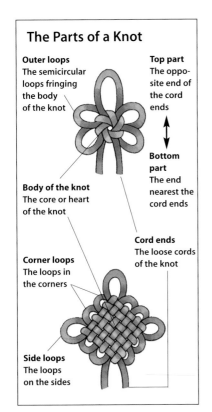

The Parts of a Knot

Outer loops
The semicircular loops fringing the body of the knot

Top part
The opposite end of the cord ends

Bottom part
The end nearest the cord ends

Body of the knot
The core or heart of the knot

Cord ends
The loose cords of the knot

Corner loops
The loops in the corners

Side loops
The loops on the sides

TIPS
• It is better to use more cord (at least 3 meters) than less so that you do not come up short at the end.
• Seal off the ends of cords with tape, thread, liquid glue or hot wax to prevent fraying.
• Make sure you keep the cord flat as you follow the step-by-step diagrams.
• String on beads, etc. at the appropriate point in the knotting process.
• Leave enough space for the cord to pass through as many times as required.
• Make sure than no bends, twists or kinks develop in the cord as you knot.
• Be patient and cautious when tightening the cords and pulling out the loops.
• Stitch the knot at relevant points (e.g. pendant junctions) to help retain the shape.

BASIC SKILLS

All Chinese knots, be they simple or compound, are based on the same underlying three-step principle: tying the knot, tightening the cord, and adding the finishing touches. Once this basic principle has been grasped and the method for making each knot mastered, all the knots you have learned can be freely recombined to produce boundless creative knots.

The fundamentals of Chinese knotting can be broken down into basic skills and formation skills. Central to the basic skills is the use of a single cord and double or multiple cords, coupled with the choice of running the cord ends separately or in parallel, to make a multitude of knots or knot formations. Formation skills involve the extension of the cord ends and outer loops, as well as the hook-up of outer loops. Using these techniques, all the knots can be hooked up into a formation to make an elegant ornament.

Making a Knot or Formation

As noted above, making a knot or formation involves three basic steps: tying the knot, tightening the cord, and adding the finishing touches. These general guidelines apply to every knot in this book and provide the foundation on which you can build your knotting skills. If you want to further enrich the knot, you can always use two, three or even more cords of different colors to make a striking multicolored ornament.

The practice of running the cord ends separately or in parallel can achieve other desirable effects. For example, using cords of different colors, with the core ends running in parallel or separately, can give rise to very colorful and elegant knots, such as round brocade, *pan chang*, cloverleaf, and good luck knots. In addition, tightening or loosening certain colored cord(s) can produce various patterns on the outer loop, thereby changing the design.

In the olden days, people used nothing but their bare fingers to hold the cord in place while tying even the most complicated of knots. These days, most knotters benefit from a few simple tools: a piece of corkboard of a shallow cardboard box on which to place the cord as the knot is formed; a number of push pins for anchoring the cords as they are knotted, perhaps in different colors for the body and loops; a crochet hook or a pair of slim tweezers for feeding the cord through narrow spaces and ensuring that the cords do not twist or bend out of shape; a pair of scissors for trimming, and a needle and different colored threads for sewing delicate and discreet stitches to ensure the knot holds its shape permanently.

Knotting a single cord

Basically all Chinese knots can be done using a single cord. The same result can be achieved by knotting one end or both ends of the cord, but as it is quite difficult to analyze the knot, beginners are encouraged to knot both cord ends to give a clearer cord path, thus avoiding confusion arising from the tying. Hence, knotting both ends of a single cord is the simplest and most convenient of all knotting skills.

Knotting one end of a single cord

When making a formation, there is, however, a need to use this particular technique for better flexibility. With frequent references to the step-by-step illustrations on basic and compound knots, starting from the last step of tightening the knot, it is easy to follow one end of the cord to trace back to the other end and make an elegant knot employing this technique. This knotting technique is frequently used to tie side knots on the outer loops, or when making necklaces and belts with Chinese knots.

Knotting both ends of a single cord

Usually, a knot tied with a single cord is made of only one color. To provide variety in the color of a formation, the ends of two different colored cords can be tied to form a single cord. Diagram 1, the cloverleaf knot, is an example. By making the join of the two different colored cords fall at the junction of the top outer loop, the two colors become evenly distributed in the body of the knot. Also, as shown by the *pan chang* knot in diagram 2, by making the join of the two different colored cords fall at the top outer loop, the two colors become evenly intertwined in the knot body and are represented equally on both sides of the knot.

Knotting Double Cords

Another way of adding color is to knot two different colored cords together as if they were one. Since two cords are being knotted together, the end result tends to be bigger and in some cases, for example the button knot, also thicker.

Knotting two cords as one

This knotting technique is normally confined to simple knots. Complicated knots when done this way, such as the *pan chang*, tend to end up messy. A better way of carrying out this technique is to tie one cord first then, before tightening the knot, tie the second cord following exactly the same path as the first cord before finally tightening both cords. If the two cords are different in color, hardness and thickness, the harder or thicker cord should always be tied first followed by the softer or thinner one. To achieve a pleasing knot, the second knot should always be kept on the right or left side of the first one, not on a mixture of both sides.

See project 124 on pages 154–155 for instructions on making the pendant above.

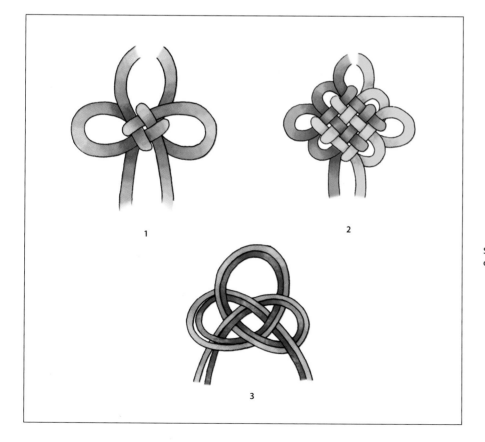

1

2

3

技法篇

基本技法

《如何設計中國結》

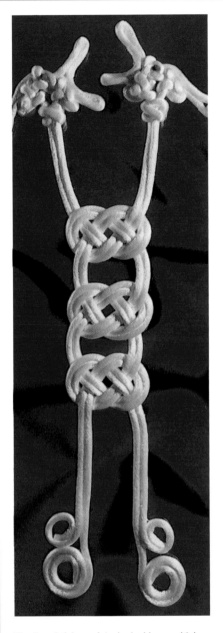

The thoughtful use of single, double or multiple cord knotting techniques, either tied as a single cord or as separate cords, can give rise to a great deal of color and stylistic variation.

See project 125, page 155, for instructions on making the knot formation above.

Knotting two cords separately

Knotting two cords as one not only produces a body comprising two different colors, but also allows one cord to be tied separately to form outer and side loops. This further enhances the combination of colors. For example, diagram 4 shows a butterfly knot tied in this way. The body of the knot was tied by knotting two cords as one. Then, as the outer loops were reached, one of the cords was tightened. The other cord was separated and tied into a butterfly wing. Another example is shown as a clover-leaf knot in diagram 5. When the outer loop was reached, one cord was tightened while the other one was pulled longer. Notice that the knot body and outer loops are of different colors as are the top outer loop and the outer loops on both sides.

Knotting Multiple Cords

The technique of knotting with multiple cords is similar to that of knotting two cords. But since more cords are involved, there is much more opportunity for experiment and variation. Added to this are the factors of cord colors and textures. The number of possible combinations that can be achieved is enormous.

Knotting multiple cords as one

The cords can get easily tangled up when knotting multiple cords as one. However, with all the different cord colors and textures involved, the entanglement might produce a unique design, much like the knot shown in diagram 6. However, if you want the end result to be like that illustrated in diagram 7, where all the different colors are lined up properly, a technique similar to that of knotting two cords as one should be

4

5

6

7

employed; that is, the thickest or hardest cord should be tied first, followed by the second cord, third cord, etc. Each cord should be inserted in its proper place in the design before all are tightened.

Knotting multiple cords separately

When knotting multiple cords as one, on reaching the outer loop one or several of the cords can be used to produce outer loops or side loops, thus adding another variation. For example, in the cloverleaf knot tied with three different colored cords in diagram 8, the three outer loops are formed of different colored cord. Similarly, in the *pan chang* knot tied with four different colored cords in diagram 9, the outer loops are highlighted with a number of color combinations. In addition, all sorts of side loops of different colors can be created with the lengthened outer loops.

The most critical part of knotting is, of course, the tightening of the knots, especially when multiple colored cords are used. It is necessary, first of all, to determine which cords are to be pulled (usually indicated by black arrows on the step-by-step diagrams). A gentle, even pressure should be applied to make sure that no twists or kinks develop. The body of the knot should always be tightened first before pulling out the slack, loop by loop, until the cord ends are reached. It is important not to let the body of the knot loosen, or its shape will be distorted.

8

9

A necklace created by the author. Once you have mastered the basic skills, you can then apply the formation skills freely to create other graceful and elegant accessories and ornaments.

See project 129 on page 157 for instructions on making this necklace.

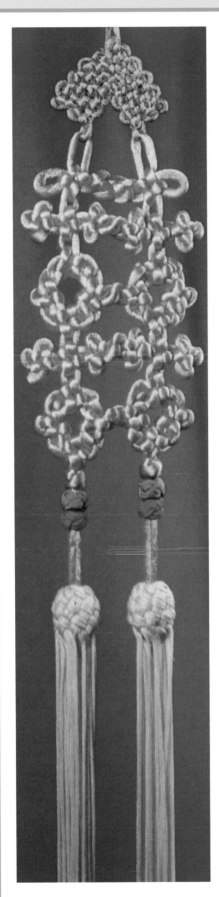

FORMATION SKILLS

A knot formation, as the name suggests, is not a single knot but a group of simple or compound knots linked together. This section focuses on the various ways of connecting the unrelated knots to make such a formation.

All compound knots and knot formations originating from simple knots follow three techniques: cord end extension, outer loop extension and outer loop hook-up. Coupled with the techniques of knotting single, double and multiple cords, as well as the skills of cord addition and reduction, it is possible to make fascinating and innovative knot formations.

Cord End Extension

The simplest and most common technique for making knot formations is the cord end extension technique. This involves using the end of a cord to tie another knot *after* a knot has already been made with one or both ends of the cord. Besides enabling the formation of a long series of knots, the technique also allows the knotter to adjust the distance between individual knots to produce a pleasing formation arrangement. This technique applies to the extension of one or both cord ends.

Extension of one cord end

The extension technique using one cord end comprises making a knot with one cord end, then making a second knot on the same cord end. In most cases, all the knots tied will fall on the same side of the cord, as shown in the cloverleaf knot in diagram 10. The few exceptions include the double coin knot as well as the button knot, as shown in diagram 11. To add variety, cords of different colors and textures can be tied using this technique.

Extension of both cord ends

The extension technique using both cord ends involves folding a cord and tying a knot using the two cord ends, as shown in diagram 12. Using both cord ends again, another knot is made. In this technique, most knots will be formed equally on both sides of the cords, with both cord ends as their centers, as shown in the cloverleaf knot in diagram 13. Variations in color and texture can be added by knotting two or more cords of different colors and textures as one single cord.

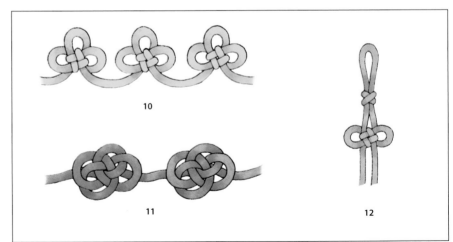

10

11

12

See projects 126 and 127 on page 156 for instructions on making the knot formations on the left and on page 15.

Application of the Extension Technique

The extension technique of using one or both cord ends together can be applied in a knot formation. The methods involved are random combination, knot body penetration and rim embellishment.

Random combination

After making a knot with multiple cords – and depending on the desired design – different cord ends can be randomly combined and the knotting continued using the extension technique of one or both cord ends. The knot formation in diagram 14 has been made by first folding four different colored cords and then tying a good luck knot, then breaking the eight cord ends into three groups of two, four and two. Each group was then tied into a knot using the extension technique of both ends. The eight cord ends were then regrouped into three groups of one, six and one. Finally, the extension techniques of one cord end, two cord ends and one cord end were used to tie the three groups into three individual knots.

Knot body penetration

When making knot formations with multiple cords, the knot body penetration technique involves pushing some cords through the knots. For example, some of the cord ends from the first knot can be used to tie a second knot, while the remaining cord ends are pushed directly through the body of the second knot to meet up with the other cord ends below. Knotting is then continued using the extension technique of one or both cord ends. However, to be able to push the cord ends through a knot body, the knot concerned must be a thick one, such as the *pan chang*, button, flat (see *Chinese Knotting*, page 58) or double connection knot. This method is normally employed when only a few cords are needed to make the second knot, and the same cords are used to make a third knot, with the non-essential cords being pushed through the second knot body, as shown in diagram 15, where double cords are used to form a knot formation.

The knot above illustrates the use of the rim embellishment method (page 16) to combine the green *ling hua* knot (page 94) with the brown side knots, at the same time embellishing the rim of the green knot.

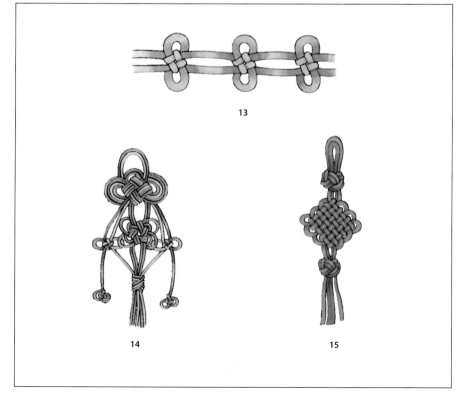

13

14

15

Rim embellishment

This method shares the same principle as the knot body penetration method in that only certain cords are used to tie a knot in the formation. The difference between them is that instead of penetrating the knot body, the cords concerned are used to decorate the rim of the knot body using the extension technique of one cord end, as shown in diagram 16. After embellishing the rim, the cord end(s) concerned can meet up with the other cord ends underneath to make other knot(s) using the extension technique of one or both cord ends.

Outer Loop Extension

The outer loop extension technique is used to make a side loop on an existing outer loop. Upon reaching the outer loop, another knot is tied on this loop, as shown in diagram 17. The side loop can also be extended to make other side loops, as shown in diagram 18. The knotter works from the inside to the outside when tying this series of side loops, although they are completed in the reverse.

Besides extending an outer loop into a side loop, two outer loops can also be used to tie a side loop. For example, on a *pan chang* knot, two outer loops can be used on the same side to tie a side loop, as shown in diagram 19; or, as shown in diagram 20, an outer loop and a corner loop can be used to tie a side loop; or, as shown in diagram 21, the outer loops from different sides can be used to tie a side loop.

Outer Loop Hook-up

This method can be used to hook up two different knots to make a formation. The method can be broken down into direct hook-up, double coin hook-up and rim embellishment hook-up.

Life can be injected into a knot formation using the extension technique of the outer loops and the hook-up technique. This knot, depicting a basket of flowers and a butterfly flirting with flowers, exhibits joy and prosperity.

See project 111 on page 149 for instructions on making this knot formation.

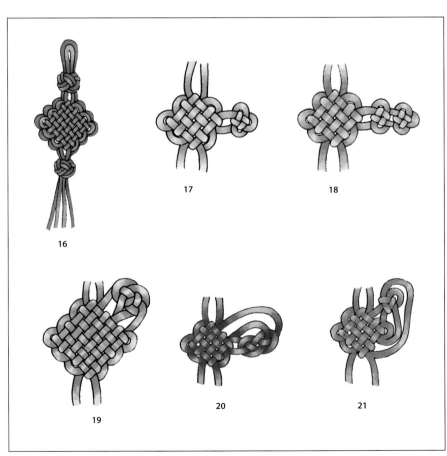

16

17

18

19

20

21

Direct hook-up

Two knots can be directly hooked up through their outer loops to create a formation or to hold them in position in the formation. Hook-up can be done through corner loops, as shown in diagram 22, or through all the outer loops, as shown in diagram 23. When extending loops, hook-up can be employed on all the extended loops to form a knot, as shown in diagram 24.

Double coin hook-up

This method is much the same as the direct hook-up, except that two knots are hooked up by tying the outer loops of the two knots into a double coin knot, as in diagram 25. To achieve this, it is necessary to first form the outer loop of the first knot into a figure eight before introducing the outer loop of the second knot into the figure to produce the double coin.

Rim embellishment hook-up

As shown in diagram 26, in the rim embellishment hook-up method, two knots are tied, then the cord ends of one knot are tied to the two sides of the other knot, thereby hooking up the two knots and achieving an embellishment effect at the same time.

See project 128 on page 157 for instructions on making this knot formation.

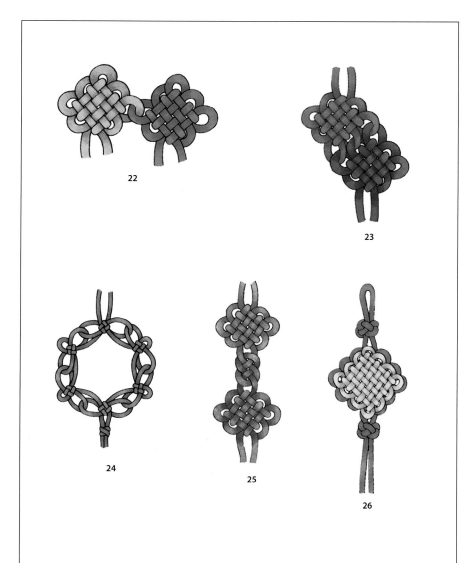

22

23

24

25

26

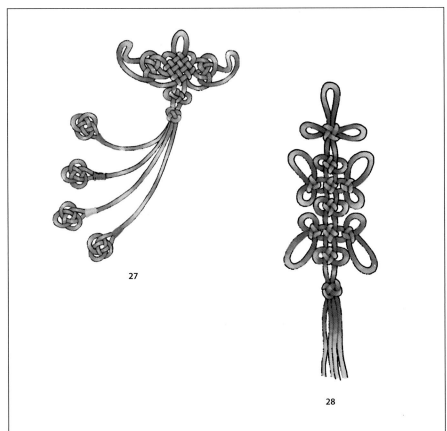

Ornament Design

It is important to consider the purpose of making an ornament before deciding on its size, form and color. It is usually helpful to draw the ornament on a piece of paper and think of which basic and compound knots could be used to make it. The four concepts below – traditional lucky designs, general design principles, application compatibility and planar (flat) options – provide guidelines on ornament design.

Traditional lucky designs

A casual glance at traditional Chinese knots tells us that the majority of them are tied with a single cord, with both sides being equal and the front and back exactly the same. They also exude auspiciousness, for example, the five happiness knot (page 86) and prosperity knot (page 99). Ornaments can also be designed with a traditional flavor. Diagram 27 shows how the butterfly knot has been modified into a bat knot and double coin knot. The ornament is named "Good Fortune Bat," denoting luck and good fortune, since bat and luck have the same sound. Diagram 28 shows how a swastika knot (*Chinese Knotting*, page 44) can be combined with a longevity knot (*Chinese Knotting*, page 64) to produce a knot named "Long Live the Good Fellow."

27

28

Chinese knots tend to follow lucky designs. Hanging a longevity tassel tied with yellow cords on a knot formation will impart good wishes.

See project 130 on page 158 for instructions on making this knot formation.

TIPS
• When making ornaments from decorative knots, it is necessary to consider the purpose and the occasion for which the ornament is being made.
• It is also important to think about the size, the most appropriate knots and the most suitable colors.
• Consider what other embellishments, e.g. tassels, beads and bindings, can be incorporated to enhance the beauty of the knots in the ornament.

要領篇

造形要領

《如何設計中國結》

General design principles

The most elegant knot formations are invariably the result of taking into account such basic design principles as balance, contrast, harmony and variety. When designing a hanging ornament, care must be given to its center of gravity. When enhancing a knot formation with a hanging ornament, it is also important to check that the knot formation can support the ornament without distorting the shape.

Application compatibility

Since a knot formation comprises a combination of two or more different knots, it is necessary to decide at the outset of a project which knots in an ornament will be the major ones and which will be the minor ones. In the example shown in diagram 29, four cloverleaf knots form the minor knots, and these are used to highlight the central *pan chang* knot, which is the major, dominant knot in the formation.

It is also necessary to consider what will be the dominant element in a formation – the knot itself or the decorative embellishment(s) – as the dominant element must be more eye-catching. Diagram 30 shows that the knot formation, enhanced by a small circular piece of jade, is the major feature. When the embellishment is to be the main design element, it must not be overshadowed by a knot formation whose purpose is merely to support and augment the embellishment. As an example, diagram 31 shows how a smaller knot can be used to grace a larger piece of agate.

Consideration must also be given to the compatibility between the knot formation and the embellishment(s). For example, hair clasps – long hanging ornaments with tassels – are designed in such a way that when the wearer walks the tassels will dangle in harmony, contributing to a graceful appearance. Diagram 32 illustrates a fan decorated with a knot formation sprouting a tassel. A woman using this fan will attract attention as the long tassel swings to the movement of her hand.

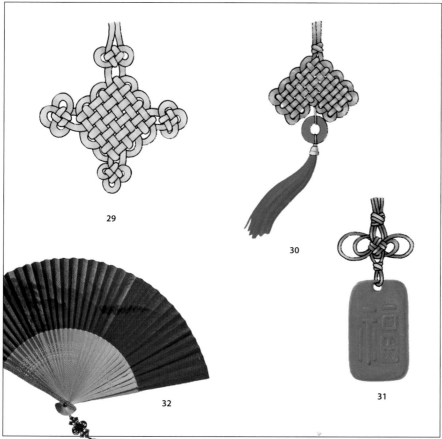

29

30

31

32

See project 131 on page 158 for instructions on making this knot formation.

造形要領

This beautifully knotted flying phoenix would look wonderful on any plain colored outfit. A series of similar formations, perhaps in different colors, could be used to decorate the corners of cushion covers or table mats. The possibilities are endless!

See project 132 on page 159 for instructions on making the phoenix.

Planar options

Traditionally, knot formations are three-dimensional hanging ornaments, but they can also be used to grace planar or flat surfaces, for example as buttons on traditional robes. A knot formation can also be sewn directly onto a garment, making a unique outfit as well as imbuing it with a touch of elegance. Diagram 33 illustrates a necktie adorned with a knot formation, adding a traditional flavor to a Western concept. It is also possible, after a knot formation has been held in place, to draw on the outer loop and bend and twist it in other ways, such as into a lively wing or a bouquet of flowers and leaves, as shown in diagram 34. In addition, a different colored cord can be bent or twisted and sewn onto the lengthened outer loop for a more pleasing aesthetic effect.

A variation on sewing the knot formation flat on a garment is to pack the space between the two surfaces with a filler such as cottonwool and then sew around the edges of the knot formation. This produces the effect of a relief sculpture.

Color Blending

A traditional knot, tied with a single cord, normally comes in a single color, as in diagram 35. Being plain and – some might say – monotonous, a single color knot often needs other knots or embellishments to enhance it. Using the basic skills, two or even three different colored cords can be tied together to produce knots like those in diagrams 36 and 37. Adding or reducing cords freely during the knotting process offers many more visually interesting options than a single color.

33

34

Principles of color blending

Most people select colors according to personal preference. However, a simple insight into the principles of color blending can intensify knotting formations.

Through a prism, sunlight can be broken down into its seven colors, namely red, orange, yellow, green, blue, indigo and violet, each having its own clarity and brightness. As shown in diagram 38, the blending of blue and yellow, with yellow being brighter and clearer than blue, produces a pleasant contrast and also emphasizes the weave pattern of the knot. Blending colors of low brightness and clarity tends to produce a harmonious effect, for example dark green and dark brown, dark purple and dark blue. For loud, eye-catching contrast, colors like yellow and purple, orange and blue or, as in diagram 39, red and light green, are best.

The matching of similar colors, for example warm colors together, such as red, orange and yellow, or cold colors together, such as blue, indigo, green and purple, tends to inject a sense of harmony and unity into a knot formation. Colors in between the warm and cold ranges, for example purple and reddish purple, as shown in diagram 40, are equally harmonious. Colors outside the normal spectrum, like black, white, gold and silver, have great potential to add interest to a knot formation as they are easy to blend with other any color.

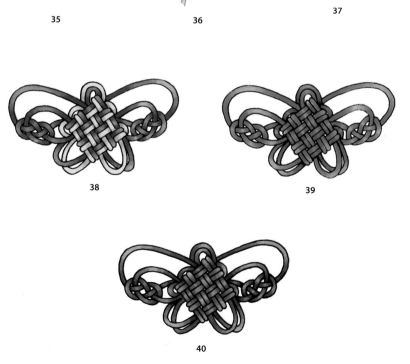

35

36

37

38

39

40

Color blending plays a central role in the design of knot formations. In this charming pendant, the blue of the stone face is carried through to the intertwining blue and gold of the stone chime knot, based on an ancient Chinese percussion instrument, to the golden side knots embedded in shiny beads – a fine display of the blending of cold colors with neutral colors and neutral colors with warm colors.

See project 48 on page 131 for instructions on making this bracelet.

● 要領篇

顏色配置

《如何設計中國結》

A white *pan chang* knot surrounded by three *ru yi* knots produces a striking contrast, much like the complementary affect of leaves and flowers. Combined with a blue-and-white porcelain vase, the whole ornament forms a serene and harmonious creation.

See project 133 on page 159 for instructions on making this ornamental hanging.

Establishing the major and minor elements

When making knot formations, not only the knots but also the colors must be divided into major and minor elements in order to provide important contrast. For example, in diagram 41, while green is the major color, by adding a touch of red to the knot body, the whole design is made to stand out. Similarly, in diagram 42, orange is the dominant color, but by highlighting the shape of the body knot with a green rim, the elegance of the whole formation is greatly enhanced. In short, a judicious and harmonious selection and mixing of colors adds aesthetic value to any knot formation.

Blending knot formations with other objects

Not only must the individual knots in a formation blend harmoniously, but they must also coordinate – as a group – with the object(s) added to the knot formation. In diagram 43, for example, the knot formation combines superbly with a beautiful piece of jade to project an image of ancient, harmonious beauty. For a more youthful and trendy look, daring colors (including luminescent ones) and everyday or unusual objects can be introduced into a design.

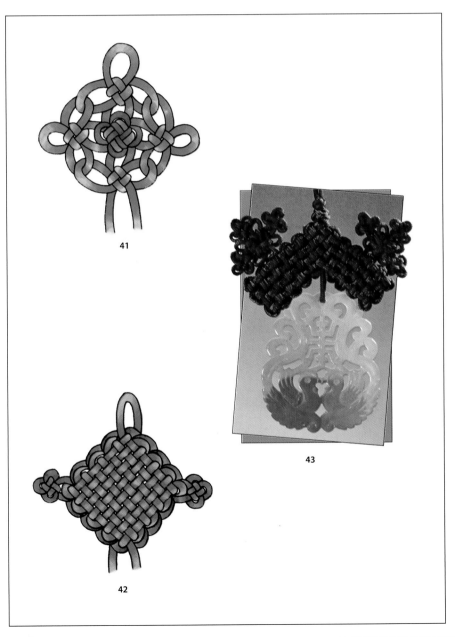

41

43

42

Embellishing Knot Formations

In addition to considering factors such as the color scheme, format and choice of cords during the initial stages of designing a knot formation, it is always a good idea to explore the possibility of incorporating small objects in the design. Such ornaments may include small hanging objects, beads, tassels, thread bindings and frames.

Hanging objects

Apart from jade or other semiprecious stones, old coins, cloth sachets, porcelain vases, porcelain and wooden sculptures, medallions and other trinkets can be used to grace a knot formation. Care must be taken, however, to ensure that the color, texture and size of the hanging object blend well with the knot formation and that it is of an appropriate size. For example, in diagram 44, the hanging ornament blends perfectly with the knot formation in terms of color, shape and size. It also fits snugly into the lower portion of the knot formation.

Beads

Jade, wood, porcelain, glass, metal and plastic beads, even love beans or fruit cores, can inject life into a knotted arrangement, their different colors, shapes, sizes and brightness adding variations and highlights. In diagram 45, green and blue beads have been added by simply pulling the cord ends through the beads at the top and bottom of the main knot, with the cords then knotted to hold them in place. Beads are also effective inserted in the outer loops of a knot, as shown in diagram 46.

See project 134 on page 160 for instructions on making this knot formation.

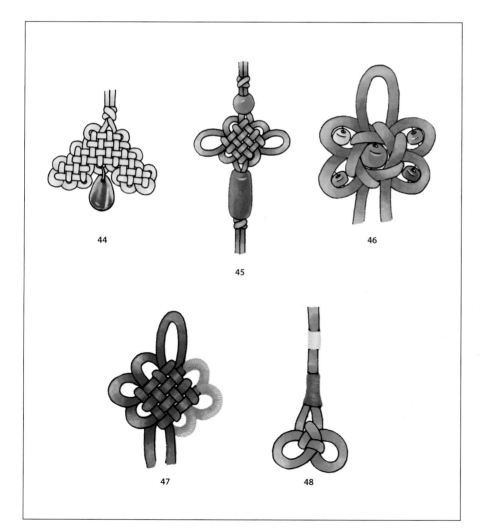

44

45

46

47

48

要領篇

配飾點綴

《如何設計中國結》

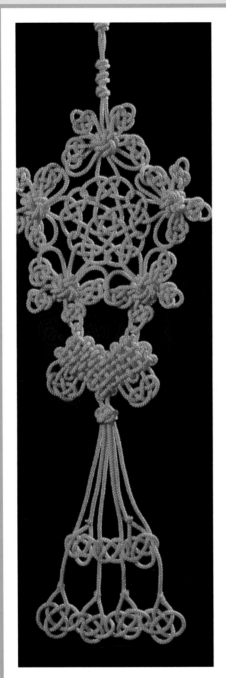

See project 135 on page 160 for instructions on making this knot formation.

Thread bindings

Thread bindings of similar or contrasting colors can both embellish and stiffen a knot formation, as shown in the outer loop in diagram 47. Binding the cord ends below a major knot is a variation on using beads or a small knot to enhance a design. Binding the join of two cord ends can both improve the appearance of a knot and hide the join. The cord ends in a tassel can also be folded back and fastened with thread or, as shown in diagram 48, the ends can be tied into a knot and then fastened with threads to the tassel cords.

Tassels

Tassels normally form the last part of an ornament and give it grace and life. Since the length of a tassel can be easily adjusted, it has a harmonious effect on the overall knot formation. There are many different types of tassels. Besides the five types taught in this book (pages 111–117), simple tassels can be made by folding back the cords and hooking them to the last knot, then tying the upper part of the tassel with threads, as in diagram 49. Alternatively, after making a knot formation, the cord ends can be tied into small knots and fastened with threads, as shown in diagram 50. Or each cord end can be strung with beads, then folded back and the cord ends bound with threads to prevent the beads from sliding down, as shown in diagram 51.

Frames

Knot formations can be held in position with jade or other rings or rattan, wood or metal frames. One way of using a frame is to line it tightly with flat knots or creeper knots. Another is to leave spaces around a central knot, as in diagram 52. The knot and frame are then linked using the outer loop hook-up technique (page 16).

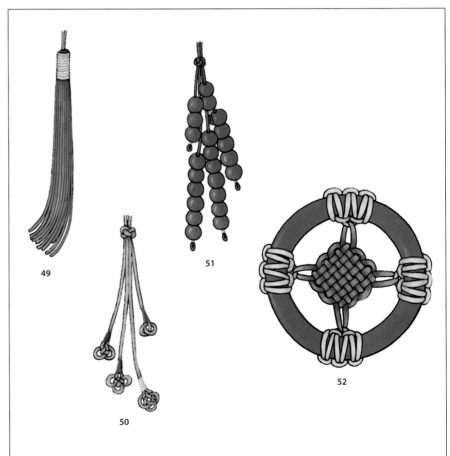

49

50

51

52

Cord Materials

Traditional Chinese knots were – and still are – made from silk or cotton cords. For the contemporary knotter, however, there are literally hundreds of types of cord to choose from: jute, hemp, twine, string, wool, leather, synthetic fiber, metal wire. In fact, anything that can be bent and tied without tearing has potential. Many materials can be found in your own home or neighborhood, while others need to be purchased from stores dealing in crafts, yarn, embroidery, macramé and tailor's supplies.

Because different materials have different textures, knot formations made from different cords will exhibit different styles and give totally different results. Because silk cords are fine, they are most suitable for classical knot formations. Cotton cords are thicker and tougher and hold their shape well. Jute cords express roughness and freedom and hence are suitable for bigger knot formations. Woolen cords have shorter fibers and tend to fray easily. They also tend not to show a clear-cut weave. Nylon and other synthetic cords are smooth and hard and tend to be loose, but if tightened properly are ideal for making stiffer knot formations. Generally, rigid cord is hard to control as it will not conform to shape. On the other hand, an overly pliant cord will not take on any shape at all. The secret lies in striking a balance between the two.

The grains in a cord will also have an impact on the visual effect of a knot. A cord with simple grains will not overshadow a knot pattern, whereas cords with complicated grains – intricately woven, unevenly textured or variegated cords – tend to detract attention from the knots themselves and muddle their patterns.

It is also important to ensure that a knot formation and the accompanying decorative objects are compatible with the cord chosen. Bigger and rougher objects go with thicker cords, small, elegant pieces with finer ones. To express grace and elegance, soft cords are ideal. To highlight a clear-cut weave, hard cords are best.

The world of Chinese knotting can be greatly enriched and enlivened by departing from the use of traditional materials such as silk and cotton cords and branching out into glossy plastic, shiny metal, natural clay and colorful cloth. The plastic cords used in the knot shown above are both stain and fire resistant. They also make a strong contemporary statement.

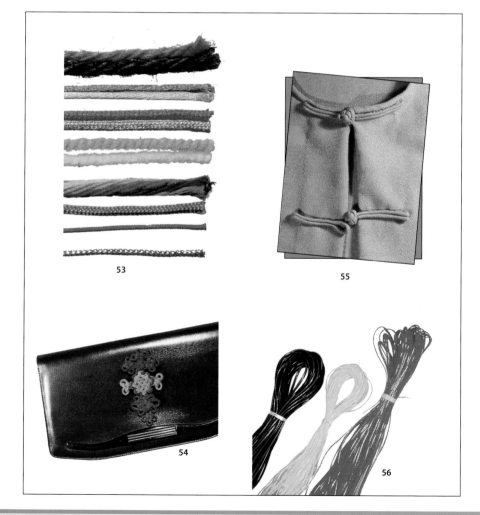

53

55

54

56

See project 50 on page 131 for instructions on making this pendant.

Leather

Leather can be formed into cylindrical strips or, as shown in diagram 54, into flat cords to make knot formations which are compatible with leather bags or other similar items. Since leather has a glossy and a rough side, a choice is available according to the needs of a particular design.

Cloth

The buttons on traditional Chinese robes, as demonstrated in diagram 55, are actually Chinese knots made from cloth. A plain color cloth is suitable for making knots for more classical attire, whereas colorful cloth can form trendy knot formations for present-day fashion wear.

Plastic

Plastic cords, shown in diagram 56, are glossy and are stain and water resistant. They can can be used to make knot formations for colorful garments, or for ornaments that frequently come into contact with water.

Metal

Metallic cords, which are stiff but do not snap when bent, can be used for making knots. Guitar strings or fuse wires that are relatively pliant, as shown in diagram 57, can be made into knot formations using one's hands alone. However, harder metallic cords such as copper wires, illustrated in diagram 58, need to be shaped with pliers.

Paper

Papers folded into long strips can be used to make knot formations, as shown in diagram 59, as a substitute for ribbon paper. Paper that does not easily crumple when rubbed, such as cotton paper, is the most suitable.

Clay

Long clay cords can be used to make simple knots, such as the one shown in diagram 60. The clay strips are formed by hand, then baked to harden them. Clay cords which are colored and then baked make for highly original knots, as in diagram 61.

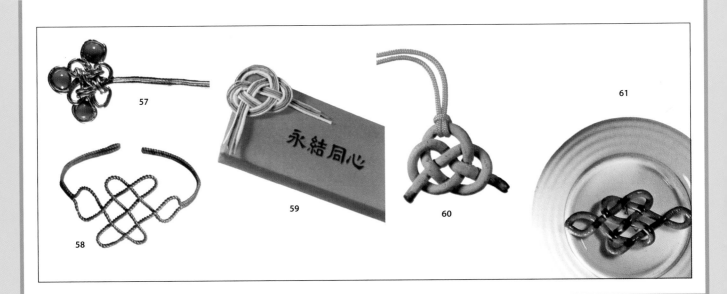

57

58

59

60

61

Living With Chinese Knots

In the past, Chinese knots were primarily used to enhance the objects they adorned, such as wind chimes, palace lanterns, spectacle cases, fans, jade pendants, seals and tobacco pouches, or were specially made as wall hangings for festive occasions and rites of passage. They were thus rather limited in their application and their beauty often went unnoticed. Even today, the items that are available on the market made with Chinese knots lack variety, and mostly comprise bracelets and belts with unimaginative designs.

This chapter makes a breakthrough in expanding the range of application of Chinese knots. It illustrates 123 innovative ways of using knots for personal adornment – as hair ornaments, hat accessories, earrings, necklaces, pendants, decoration on clothes and footwear, belts, bracelets and rings – as well as accents on other items in daily use. The section is followed by instructions for making nine basic knots and nineteen new compound knots as well as five tassels to embellish the knots.

Readers can browse through these new designs and refer to the illustrations on pages 118–154 to learn how to make them. With the assistance of the principles in designing discussed in the last section, you may be inspired to design new creative knots and further enrich our world of Chinese knotting.

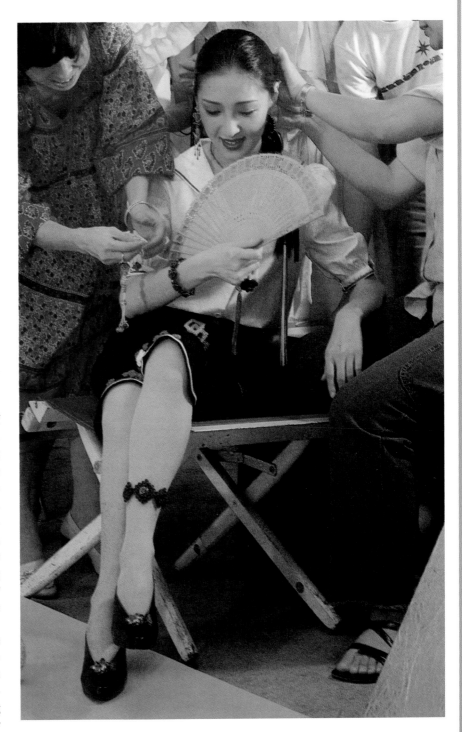

Chinese knots can add a touch of Oriental delicacy to even the latest fashions, subtly enhancing the appeal of anything they grace. More than mere eye-catchers, many are ripe with symbolic connotations, expressing wishes for good fortune and wealth and the joys of matrimony.

HAIR ORNAMENTS

Not only can we decorate hairpins with Chinese knots, we can make our own stylish hair clasps with them. We can also use our own hair as cords and tie strands into Chinese knots, thereby establishing a new hair fashion.

See the instructions on pages 120–122 for making the hair ornaments shown on these two pages.

1

2

3

5

6

7

8

9

10

11

The hairpin above is made from gold-plated fuse wire.

12

13

14

HAT ACCESSORIES

See the instructions on pages 122–123 for making the hat accessories shown on this page.

15

16

17

18

19

20

21

Disco headbands like the one below are made from plastic cords.

22

Two types of ear ornaments can be made with Chinese knots. One comprises a single "stud," the other a dangling knot formation.

See the instructions on page 124 for making the earrings on this page.

EARRINGS

23

24

25

NECKLACES

Short necklaces are best composed of a series of small, regular knots. Any additional dangling knot formation or other decorative item, such as a porcelain pendant, are also best kept small. A hook and ring on each end secures the necklace.

See the instructions on page 125 for making the necklaces shown on this page.

26

27

28

Knotted pendants can be suspended from chains or cords that are long enough to slip over the head. Generally, the knot formations on pendants can be much larger than those on short necklaces.

See the instructions on pages 126–131 for making the pendants on pages 33–37.

30

31

29

Beads strung on the ends of cords form a different type of tassel from the ones taught on pages 112–117.

32

Beads inserted inside loops, in the center of knot formations or on the ends of cords add elegance and interest to the knot formations in pendants.

39

40

41

42

43

45

46

This pendant is made from two knots in the shape of a ram's head and an axe, which denote luck.

44

A gold medallion is a perfect foil in the center of a *hui ling* knot.

47

49

48

The bluish gray
porcelain medal-
lion goes well
with the color
and texture of
the leather knot.

50

Perfect harmony is achieved in this pendant
formation tied with green and gold cords
above a golden green gemstone.

CLOTHING ACCENTS

Knot formations on clothes make for unique creations. Because the knots are flat and are supported by the surface cloth, they can be placed asymmetrically for a more interesting effect.

See the instructions on pages 132–141 for making the clothing accents shown on pages 38–44.

51

This evening gown, made of boldly contrasting colors, is enhanced with an irregular custom-designed knot formation placed around one half of the neckline for maximum effect.

52

The butterfly knot on this evening gown was deliberately curled to suit the shape of the neckline.

53

54

The clothes on page 38–44 were specially designed by Pan Daili to make the most of the knotted accents.

A knotted phoenix on the front of this short coat and a sun motif on the left shoulder add both drama and vivacity to the garment.

56

55

A flower knot formation made from leather cords harmonizes beautifully with the color and texture of the woolen sweater.

58

57

60

62

61

63

A fascinating selection of knotted buttons and fasteners (Nos. 60–71) and other chest ornaments (Nos. 72–76).

59

68

70

69

71

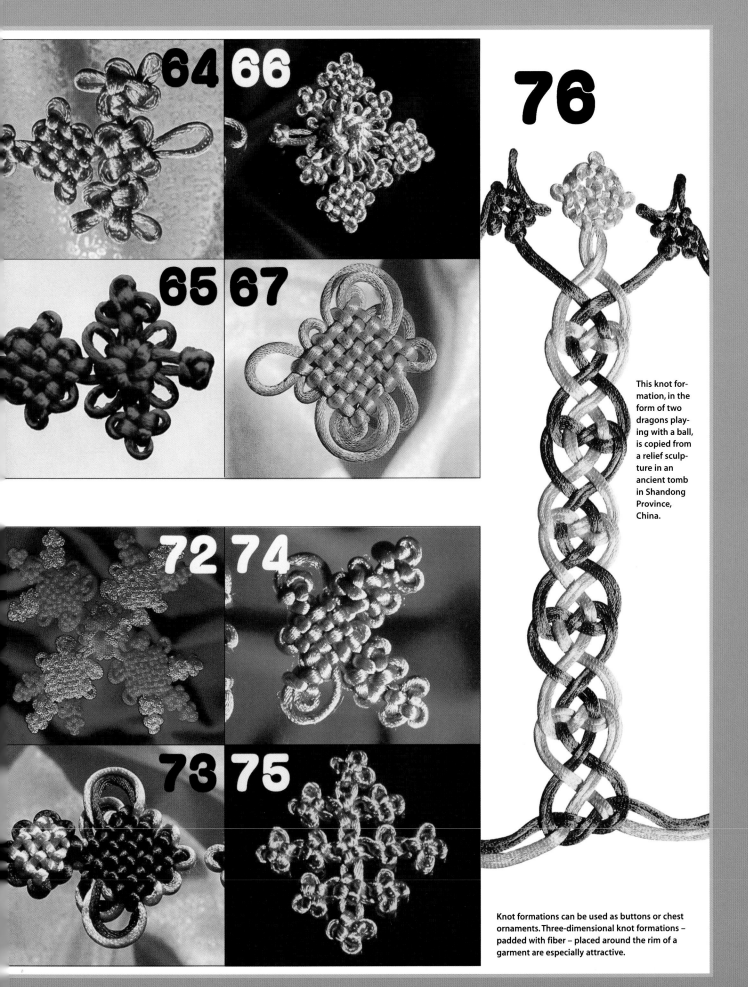

64

66

65

67

72

74

73

75

76

This knot formation, in the form of two dragons playing with a ball, is copied from a relief sculpture in an ancient tomb in Shandong Province, China.

Knot formations can be used as buttons or chest ornaments. Three-dimensional knot formations – padded with fiber – placed around the rim of a garment are especially attractive.

77

79

78

The butterfly knot here is printed straight onto the T-shirt.

80

81

82

Traditionally, flowing Chinese robes were held shut with knotted sashes. Nowadays, there is more variety. Three types of belts with decorative knotwork are shown here: one is a commercially bought belt embellished with hanging knot formations; the second is a knotted belt secured at the ends with a button knot and loop; and the third is a knotted belt with a tassel and other decorative knotwork at the ends.

See the instructions on pages 141–144 for making the belts shown on pages 45–47.

83

84

A knotted belt secured around the waist.

85

Two sets of knot formations can slide along the separately made cord-like belt.

87

88

86

A knot formation tied
to each end of a belt.

A knot forma-
tion can either
be tied to a belt
or sewn straight
onto a garment.

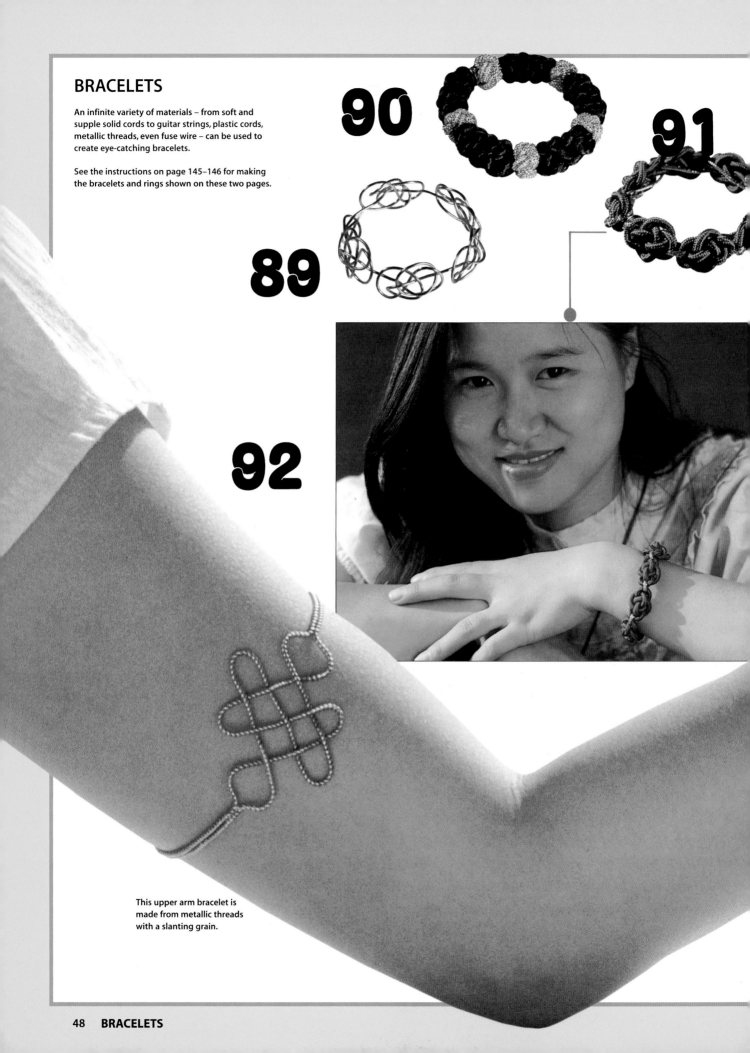

BRACELETS

An infinite variety of materials – from soft and supple solid cords to guitar strings, plastic cords, metallic threads, even fuse wire – can be used to create eye-catching bracelets.

See the instructions on page 145–146 for making the bracelets and rings shown on these two pages.

90

91

89

92

This upper arm bracelet is made from metallic threads with a slanting grain.

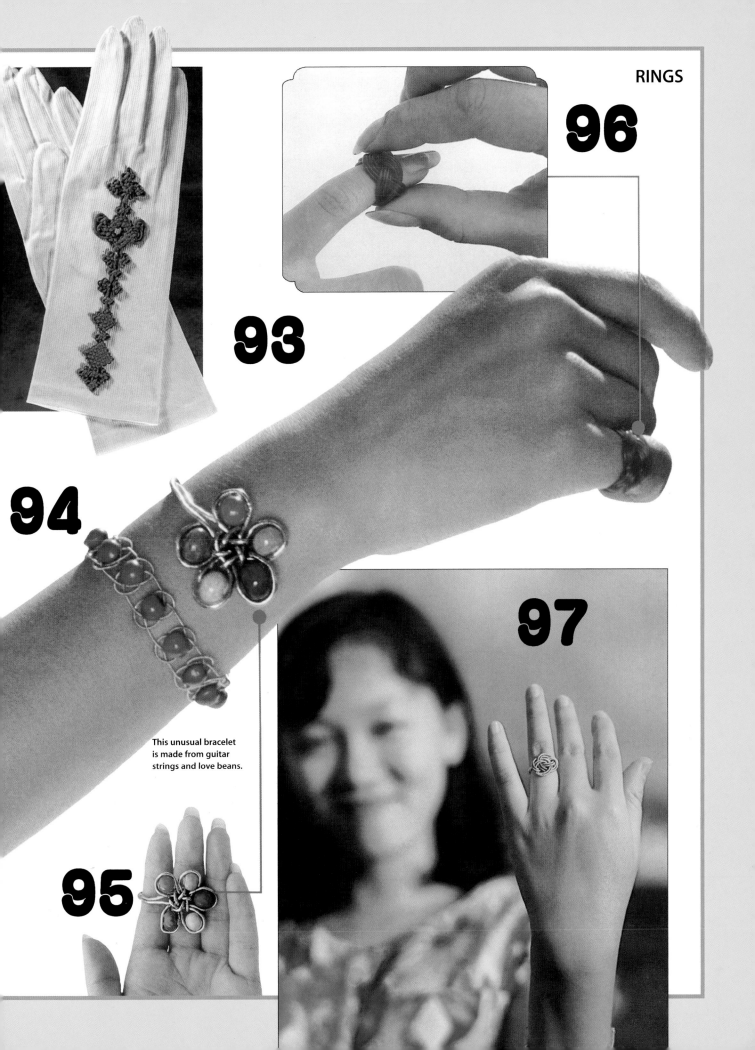

96

93

94

97

This unusual bracelet is made from guitar strings and love beans.

95

FOOTWEAR ACCENTS

Not only socks, but sandals, pumps and boots can be decorated with knot formations made from suitable cord materials.

98

99

100

101

See the instructions on page 146 for making the footwear accents shown on this page.

102

The top part of this shoe is made from a knot formation.

106

103

104

105

Decorating items in our daily lives with knot formations created from special cord materials make Chinese knots a truly living art.

OTHER DECORATIONS

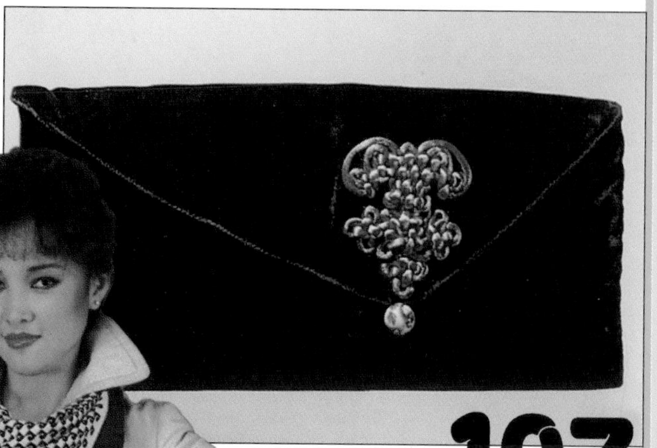

107

108

109

See the instructions on pages 147–154 for making the ornamental accents shown on pages 51–54.

110

111

112

113

114

116

A water-resistant plastic knot tied to the handle-bars can give individuality to a bicycle.

115

117

118

119

120

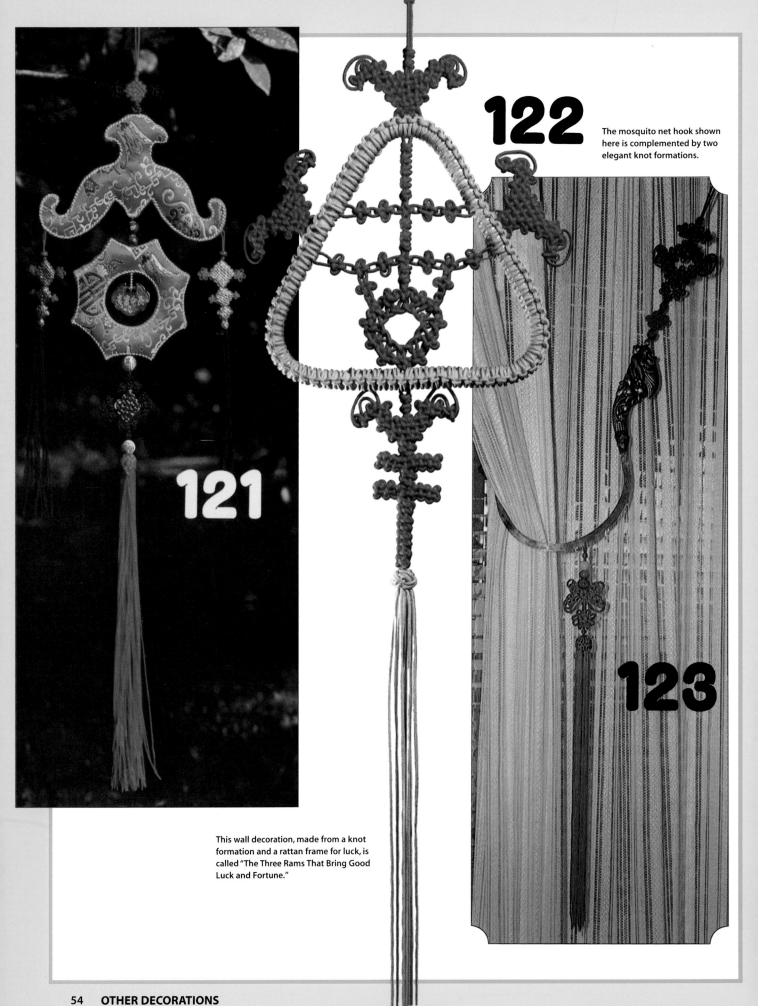

122

The mosquito net hook shown here is complemented by two elegant knot formations.

121

123

This wall decoration, made from a knot formation and a rattan frame for luck, is called "The Three Rams That Bring Good Luck and Fortune."

Basic Knots

In this section, seven of the most essential basic knots taught in *Chinese Knotting: Creative Designs That Are Easy and Fun!* (Tuttle Publishing, 2003) are repeated, and are augmented by a further two basic knots. In ancient times, Chinese decorative knotting was an oral tradition, in which the techniques were handed down from generation to generation. It is not surprising then that the origins of some knots are shrouded in mystery while others have simply been lost to time. The basic knots in both books were created by analyzing and combining ideas presented in ancient books and on historical artifacts such as bronze vessels and earthenware jugs. Some basic knots are clearly representations of traditional auspicious symbols. Others have a unique historical history. Yet others are merely technical devices used in larger knot formations.

Button Knot

The interesting little buttons found on traditional Chinese dresses and jackets are a mystery to many people. They are, in fact, formed from a simple knot. The knot can be used in conjunction with other flat-lying knots to make a variety of unusual and attractive clothes fasteners, a sampling of which is shown on pages 42–43.

Tying

Steps one and two are almost the same as for the double coin knot (page 60), with the cord going under the last loop on the right instead of over. This cord is then strung over and through the center of the knot in step 3. Step 4 brings the other end of the cord around the left side, through the top loop from underneath, and down through the center of the knot. The knot is tightened in two stages. First, pull the two loose cord ends downward while pushing the knot itself up. Then work out the slack from the upper loop by pulling it through the knot. To make a button knot that lies flat, pull the two loose ends in opposite directions during tightening, as in the inset.

Tips

• If the knot becomes distorted when you tighten it, simply pull any of the cord segments through the knot in one direction. The shape will reappear as the knot closes.
• Once you have mastered this knot, you should learn how to tie it using only one end of the cord. Many of the later knot formations require this.

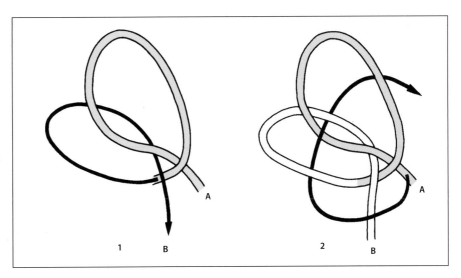

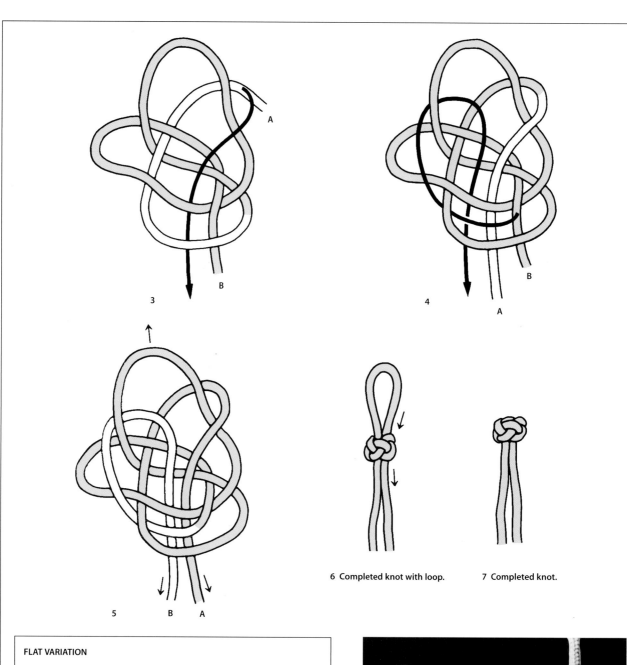

3

B

A

4

B

A

5

B A

6 Completed knot with loop.

7 Completed knot.

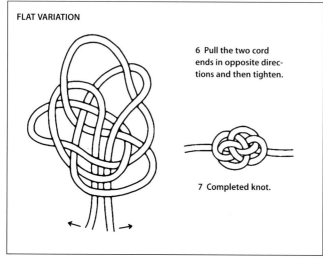

FLAT VARIATION

6 Pull the two cord ends in opposite directions and then tighten.

7 Completed knot.

Button Knots

Cloverleaf Knot

Chinese children have played a pulling game with clover leaves for generations. Some have even popped the plant into their mouths, discovering that the leaves and stalk are slightly sour, and reporting that certain varieties alleviate coughing when you have a scratchy throat. Just as in the West, good luck is said to go hand in hand with the discovery of the four-leaf variety.

Tying

One loop is formed, another is formed and passed through it, and a third one is formed and passed through the second one. The cord end is then woven through these loops and pulled together to form the body of the knot. The cord sections between these inner loops make up the outer loops of the knot. This knot can be tied with virtually any number of outer loops. Follow steps 1 and 2 but form more loops before proceeding to step 3 which pulls them to the center. The inset shows the same principles used to form a cloverleaf knot with only two outer loops.

Tips

• After the body of the knot is tightened and you are pulling the slack out of the outer loops, make sure that you hold the body securely while sliding the cord through it, otherwise the knot will come undone and be difficult to repair.
• The diagrams show how to tie the cloverleaf using only one cord end. It is essential that you learn how to do this since the knot is required in many compound knots. It also makes it easy to add cloverleaf knots to the outer loops of other knots, lending contrast and intricacy to their designs.

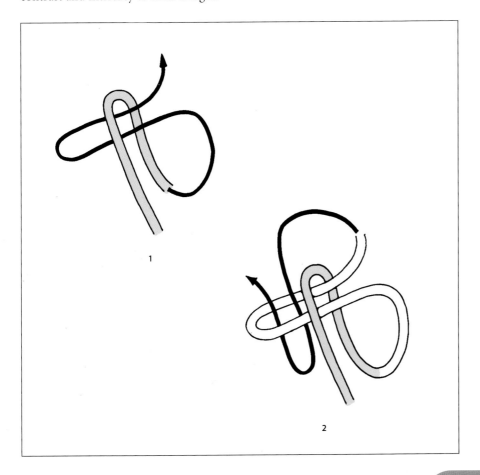

1

2

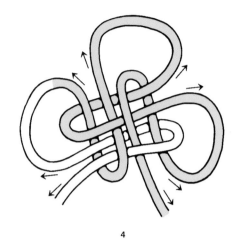

3

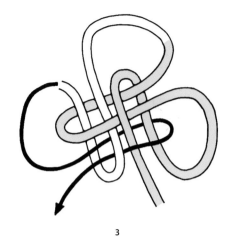

4

5 Completed knot.

Cloverleaf Knots

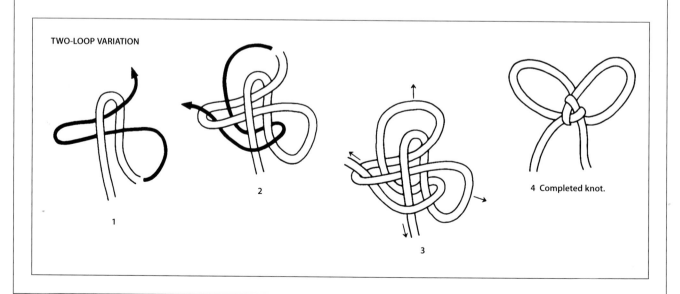

TWO-LOOP VARIATION

1

2

3

4 Completed knot.

Creeper Knot

This knot comprises a creeper outer loop and two side loops. Normally, this knot is made by tying the cord around a stiff cylindrical rod or ring-like structure which forms the axis, hence the name creeper knot. If it is not wound round an axis, the creeper loop is easily pulled out and the whole knot loosened. Tying a side loop on the creeper loop tends to stabilize it.

Tying

When tying a long series of creeper knots, ensure that the two outer loops are on different sides of the knot so that the creeper knots are not wound too tightly around the axis. If both outer loops are placed to one side of the knot, the cord cannot wind around the axis properly and will leave gaps of fixed sizes, giving rise to a completely different type of creeper arrangement.

Tip

• When making a belt with a series of creeper knots, it is best to start from the mid-section of the cord and work towards both ends in order to avoid confusion arising from working with a very long cord.

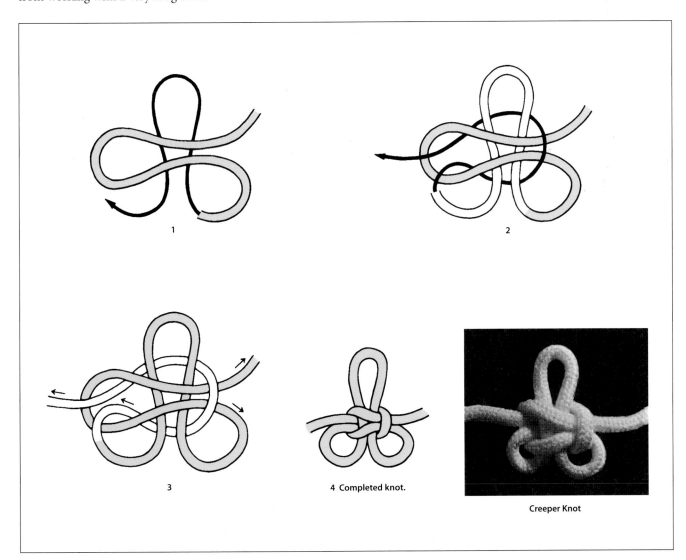

1

2

3

4 Completed knot.

Creeper Knot

Double Coin Knot

The double coin knot is a representation of an often-employed decorative motif composed of two antique Chinese coins overlapping one another. Merchants once took the design to mean prosperity, hanging it over the entrances to their shops hoping to attract wealth. Used elsewhere, the double coin motif connotes not only prosperity but also longevity.

Tying

In tying the double coin knot, two loops are made, one above the other. Then a third loop is made and is woven through the other two to hold them together. The final knot should not be tightened too much. Leave plenty of space within it to bring out its pattern.

Tips

• As this is a very loose knot, it is necessary to stitch it together where the cord crosses over itself to keep it from slipping out of shape.
• To tie this knot with one cord end, simply form two overlapping loops and weave the end back through the center. If your second loop is formed below the first, the situation is reversed.

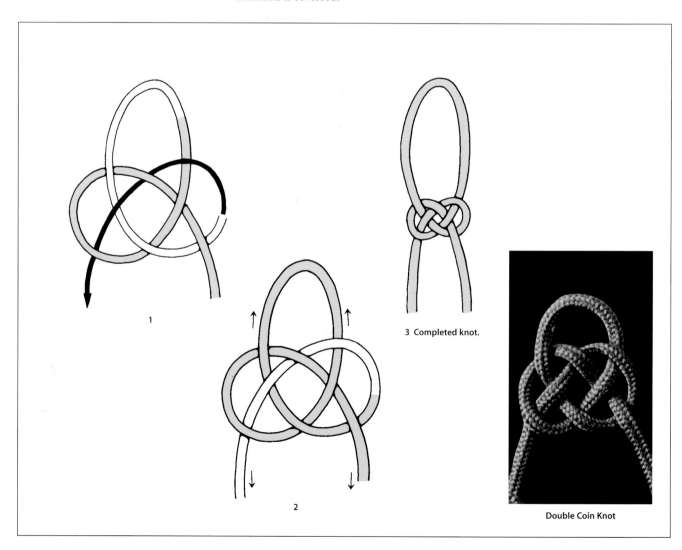

1

2

3 Completed knot.

Double Coin Knot

Double Connection Knot

The double connection knot is exactly what its name suggests – two knots tied into one another. Half of one simple knot forms half of the other.

Tying

In this very stable knot, one cord end is used to tie one simple knot around the other cord end. Then the other cord end is used to tie a simple knot around the first cord end, linking through the loop of the first simple knot. The "x" pattern will appear naturally if the cord is pulled from both top and bottom with equal force.

Tip

• Keep in mind the desired size of the top loop, or the space between the double connection knot and the knot tied before it. The loops will become much larger than they seem before tightening.

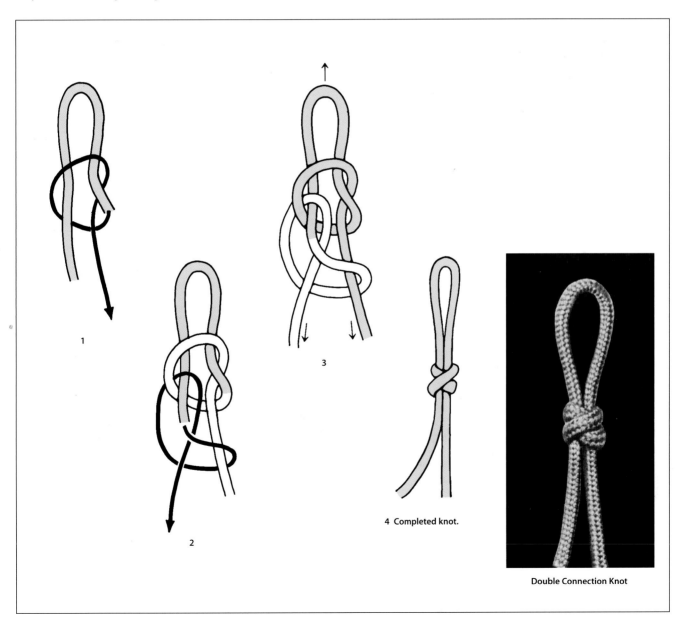

1

2

3

4 Completed knot.

Double Connection Knot

Good Luck Knot

Unlike the majority of knots whose names derive from the decorative motifs they represent, this often-seen knot was a nameless orphan. Here it is called the good luck knot, in keeping with the names of its many auspicious sister knots. It is hoped that the knot will bring good fortune to knotter and wearer alike.

Tying

This knot affords almost endless variation. It can be tied with three, four, five, six or even more outer loops. If careful attention is paid to the tightening process, it can be tied with compound petals – a small circle of loops in between the large outer ones. To start the knot, lay out the cord with as many elongated loops as you want in the finished product. (For reasons of space, the loops in diagrams 1–3 are not as long as they actually need to be to tie the knot.) Cross these loops over each other in the same direction and pull them to secure them – but not too tightly or the smaller loops will not appear later on. Then repeat the process in the opposite direction. When the knot is finished, the cord ends will be off-center. If you want to hang a pendant from the knot or proceed with another knot, follow alternate steps 4 and 5 in the inset in order to make a balanced good luck knot.

Tip

• It is hard to control the knot when the number of outer loops is more than four or five. It helps to stitch them in place before beginning step 2. After finishing step 2 and pulling the cords secure, you can remove the stitches.

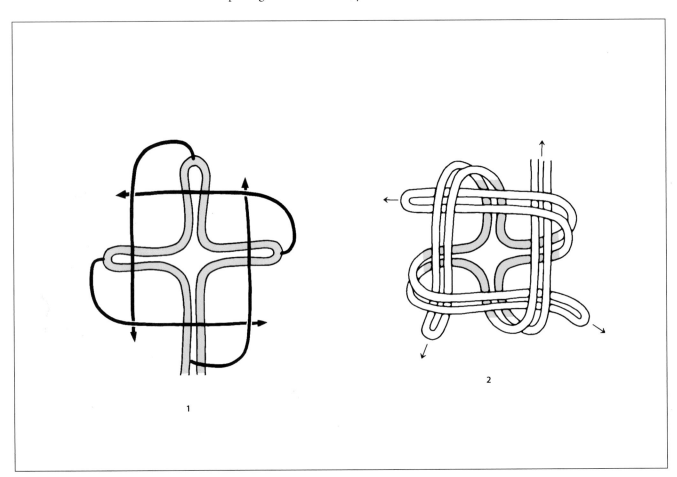

1

2

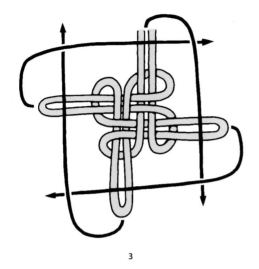

3

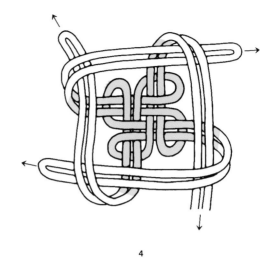

4

5 Completed knot.

BALANCED VARIATION

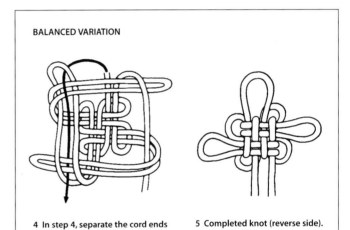

4 In step 4, separate the cord ends and pass the left loop through the top one, as shown.

5 Completed knot (reverse side).

FIVE-PETAL VARIATION

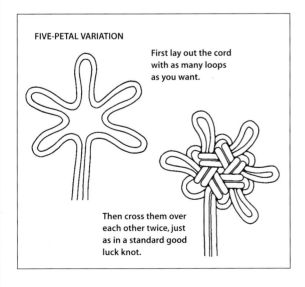

First lay out the cord with as many loops as you want.

Then cross them over each other twice, just as in a standard good luck knot.

Good Luck Knots

Pan Chang Knot

The *pan chang* or mystic knot is one of the eight Buddhist treasures. It twists and turns around itself in a seemingly endless pattern, a graphic representation of the cyclical nature of all existence. The *pan chang* knot embodies this concept, one of the basic precepts in Chinese Buddhism.

Tying

In this very stable knot, the cord is woven into a double-thickness square pattern, the warp and weft of which can be increased to make the knot as large as you want. Pay close attention to the weaving in step 3 because an understanding of this will come in handy when you tie any of the *pan chang* variations. Here, the cord from the corner loop goes under one cord, over three, under one and over three again. It turns back, goes under two, over one, under three, over one and under one to form another outer loop before repeating the whole process. Although the specific "overs" and "unders" will not be exactly the same in every variation, the underlying principle is the same: on the way up, the cord goes over everything except the pairs of cords that form the inner loops on the edge of the knot's body. Here, the mobile cord goes under the first cord of each pair. On the way back down, the pattern is reversed: the cord goes under everything, again except for the pairs that form the inner loops on the left. In these places it goes over the same ones it went over on the way up.

Tips

• Do not tighten the body of the knot too much or it will be impossible to take the slack out of the outer loops without distorting the pattern.
• To make sure that the final knot is of a regular shape and that the two cord ends are the same length, take the slack out starting from the top loop and working in both directions. After you finish in one direction, turn the knot over so that you can pull the slack through in the other direction with the same hand. This helps ensure that the same force will be applied in both directions.

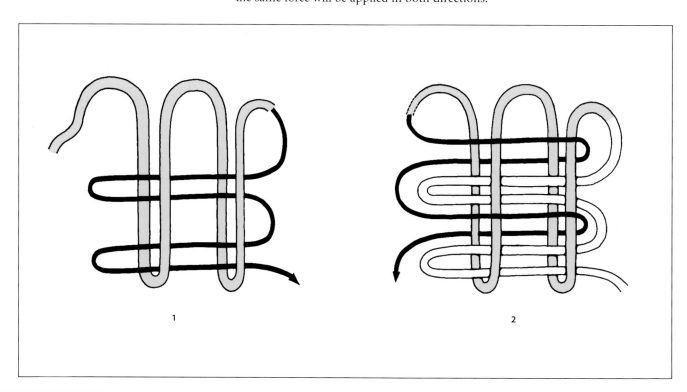

1   2

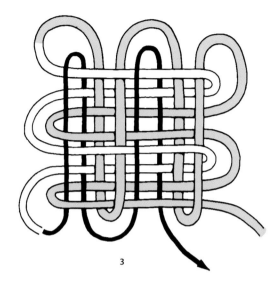

3

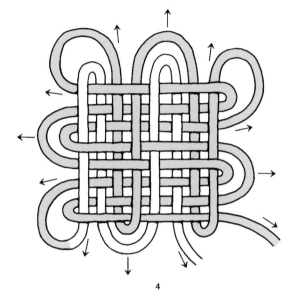

4

5 Completed knot.

Pan Chang Knot

Round Brocade Knot

This knot takes its inspiration from the round patterns often seen on Chinese brocade. A close look at the roundels reveals that they are often abstract representations of auspicious animals or characters: the dragon, the crane, the character for longevity, and the like. The fact that they are worked into a round pattern further enhances the message of good fortune, because the circle represents completeness to the Chinese.

Tying

In this knot, the outer loops are bound together by passing through each other's centers in a circular pattern. Cord A makes two horizontal passes, going under everything right to left, and over everything left to right. Then it travels up under everything to pass through the top loop, and down over everything to take its final position. Cord B's travels will be easier to grasp if you imagine the portion that comes straight down from the top loop is the knot's spine. After going up through the inner loops on the left, cord B passes through the knot twice horizontally. On each pass, when it travels left to right, it goes over everything except the spine and the cords crossing over and under the spine. When it travels right to left, it passes under every cord except the last two – the ones that it came over to begin the pass, thus returning to its origin.

Tips

• Notice that cord A forms the top loop and the two on the right, while cord B forms the two on the left, and that the cords always move away from the top of the knot when they form a loop.
• Eventually, for some of the creative applications in the back of this book, you will have to learn to tie this knot using only one mobile cord end. Follow step 7 diagram very carefully.

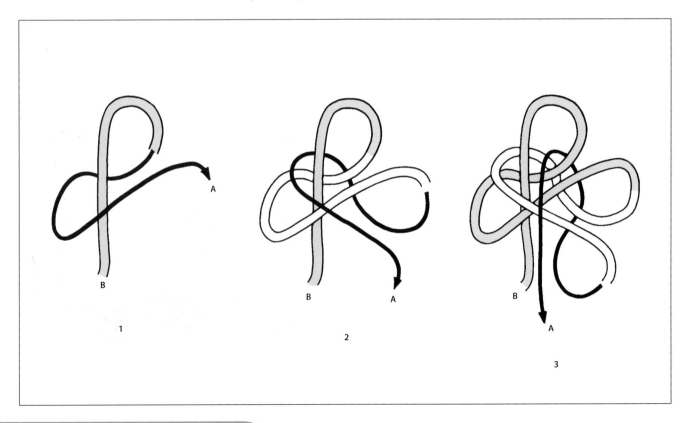

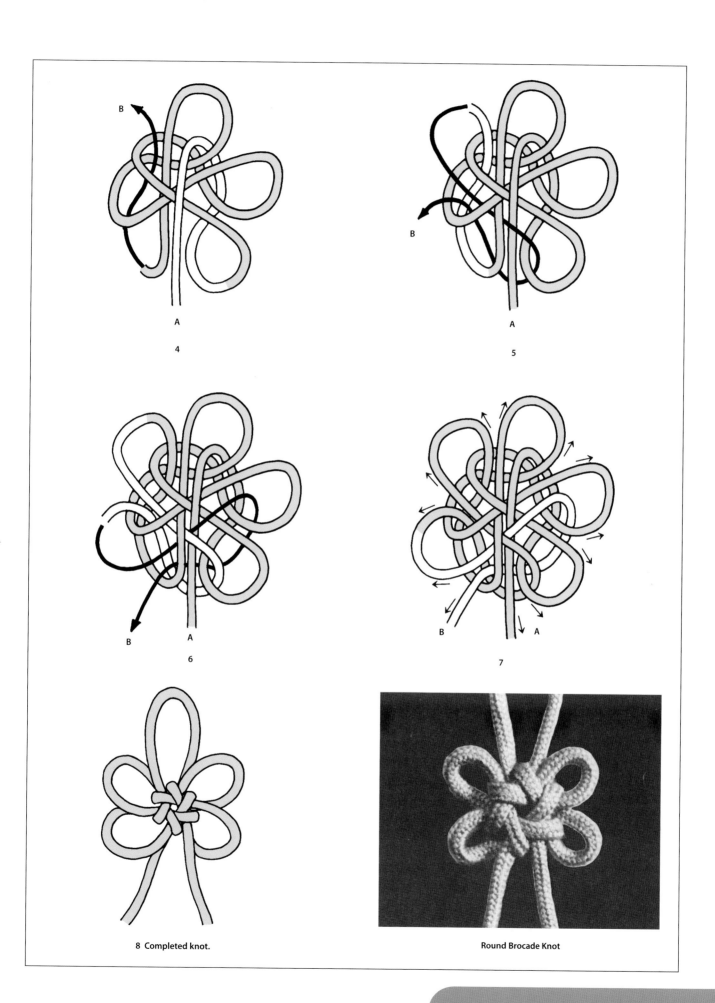

4

5

6

7

8 Completed knot.

Round Brocade Knot

Tassel Knot

On the back of Tang Dynasty mirrors, it is common to find the design of a phoenix with a tassel hanging from its beak. This knot is frequently found in tassels and hence the name tassel knot. As the front and back of a tassel knot are different, only one side is suitable for display. Though the front of the knot body appears to be a cloverleaf knot (page 57) tied with double cords, with the outer loops on both sides seemingly double-layered as well, the tassel knot is, in fact, tied with only one cord.

Tying

Tighten the two layers of the outer loop into different sizes to give the appearance of a double-layered structure. Alternatively, tie each layer of the outer loop into different knots, again to give a three-dimensional effect. If you want to attach an ornament to the knot, pull the cord end through the ornament first and then tie it.

Tips

• Keep the cord flat to avoid entanglement.
• Always adjust the cord ends and the top outer loop during the tightening process.

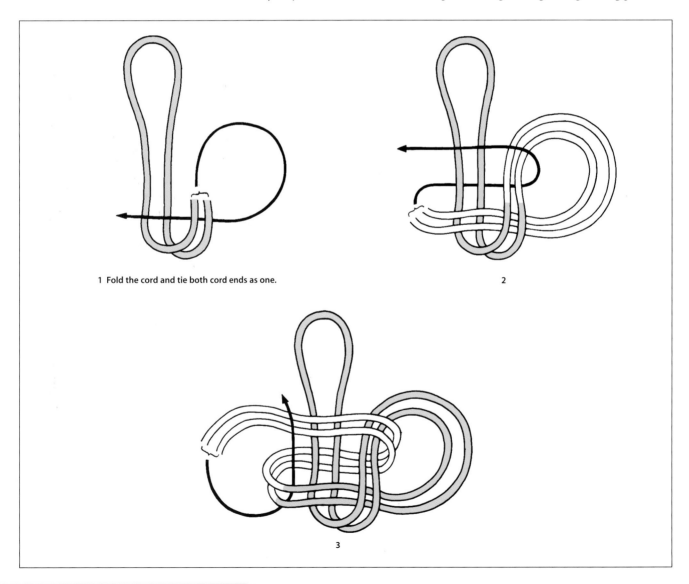

1 Fold the cord and tie both cord ends as one.

2

3

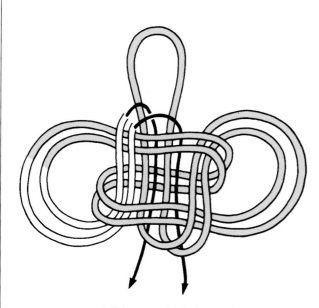

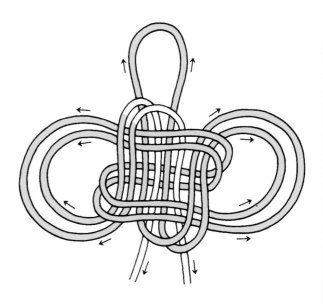

4 Pull the two cord ends downward in two separate paths.

5

Front

Back

6 Completed knot.

Tassel Knot

Compound Knots

A compound knot is either a combination of basic knots or variations of their designs, brought together to form a more complex and symbolically significant configuration drawn from nature, folk imagery and the Chinese language itself. Creating a compound knot from a basic knot, or applying the methods of extension and hook-up of outer loops with basic knots, allows the knotter to produce unlimited variations and also to invent new types of knots.

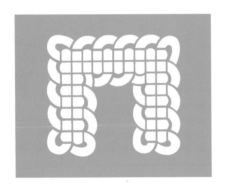

Bao Men Knot

This knot is door-shaped, hence the name *bao men*, meaning "precious door." Based on the *pan chang* knot (page 64), it is formed by tying a vertical *pan chang* knot to each end of a central, horizontal *pan chang* knot. The door space in the middle is suitable for attaching objects or for tying a tassel.

Tying

To tie the horizontal *pan chang* knot, use the technique of knotting both ends as a single cord (see page 13 above). Then, to tie each of the two vertical *pan chang* knots, use the technique of knotting one end of a single cord (see page 12 above). The length of the horizontal and vertical *pan chang* knots can be adjusted according to preference.

Tip

• During the tightening process, start with the outer loops in the middle of the horizontal *pan chang* knot before working outward to the ends and the vertical knots.

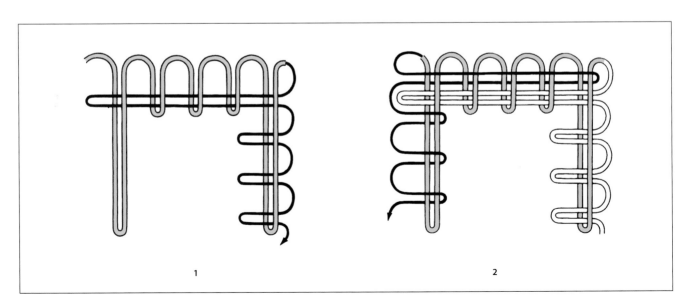

1

2

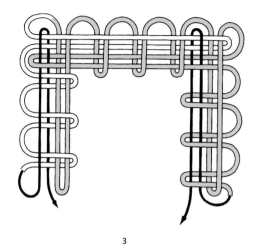

3

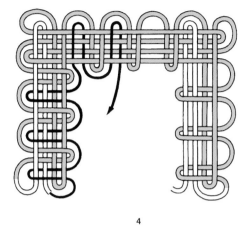

4

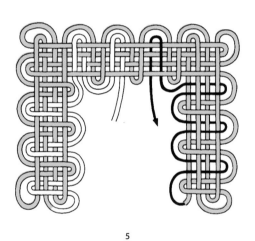

5

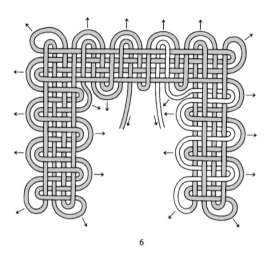

6

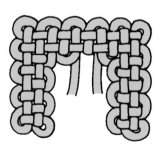

7 Completed knot.

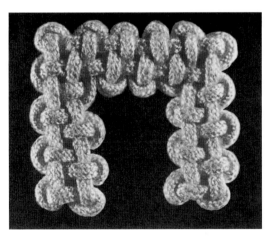

Bao Men Knot

Butterfly Knot

One night Chuang Chou dreamt he was a butterfly, flying through the air, totally at ease, unaware of his existence as a man. But when Chuang awoke, much to his surprise he found he was still a man. Did Chuang dream that he was a butterfly? Or did a butterfly dream it was Chuang? Or do the very concepts "butterfly" and "Chuang" create arbitrary divisions in the singularity that gives rise to all things? The butterfly in this parable intimates the essential oneness of all being, a basic tenet of Taoist philosophy.

Tying

The body of the butterfly knot is a simple *pan chang* knot (page 64). In the course of tying, the cord travels through two of the *pan chang*'s outer loops to form a double coin knot (page 60) at the corner. The process is repeated at the opposite corner. These double coin knots serve as the butterfly's wings while the remaining outer loops make up the head and the lower wing tips.

Tip

• Tighten the *pan chang* and double coin knots completely before taking out the slack. When you take out the slack, rotate the double coin knots in opposite directions so that the two outer loops will be at the top rather than the bottom.

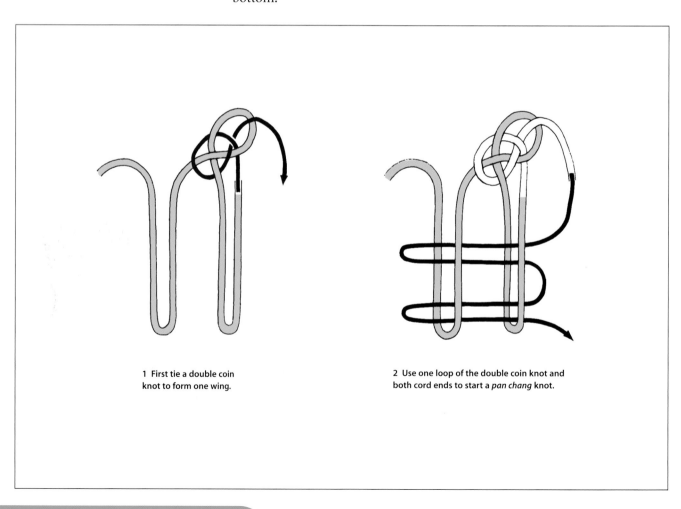

1 First tie a double coin knot to form one wing.

2 Use one loop of the double coin knot and both cord ends to start a *pan chang* knot.

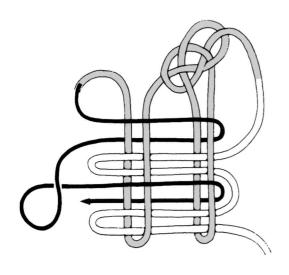

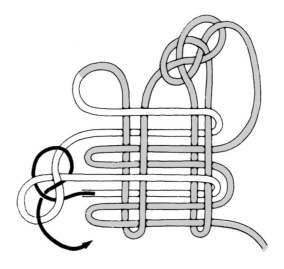

3 Now tie the other double coin knot so that it mirrors the first one.

4

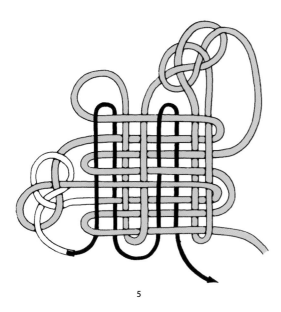

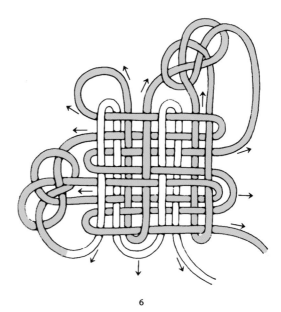

5

6

7 Completed knot.

Butterfly Knot

Button Ring Knot

This knot has the same basic shape and structure as the button knot except that it now has a hollow center, hence the name button ring knot. When a string is passed through the center of the knot, the whole knot can slide freely along it. It can thus be used as a decorative design to replace beads. It can also be used to cover the join of two cords.

Tying

One cord is used to tie this knot. Using a cylindrical rod as the axis, wind the cord clockwise twice around the rod from the bottom up. Hold cord end B steady with the left thumb and use cord end A at the top for tying. Pull up the bottom cord on the side of the rod to intersect with the top cord, as shown in step 2, then weave cord end A into and around the intersection. Part 1 is then completed. Next, turn the axis slightly clockwise and start winding the cord around the rod again, as described in part 1. Follow this method and tie as many parts as you like in accordance with the length of the rod and the length of the cord. If you tie cord end A backwards to follow the original route, the whole thing will become a double-layered structure. If you make another round following this same method, it will become a triple-layered structure. Finally, pull out the rod axis and sew the cord ends into the body of the knot.

Tips

• As cord end B is not tied, keep it short and steady on the axis.
• After the tying process is completed, tighten the cord as much as possible so that when the axis is pulled out, each part of the knot is exactly the same.

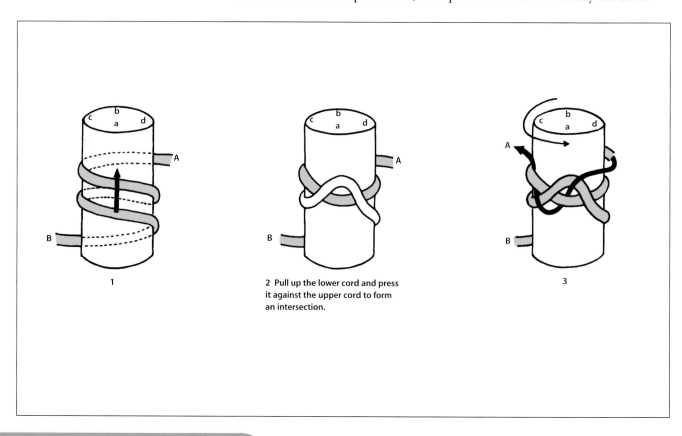

1

2 Pull up the lower cord and press it against the upper cord to form an intersection.

3

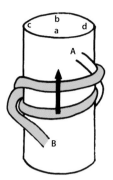

4 Turn the axis clockwise slightly and repeat steps 2 and 3 to complete part 1 of the button ring knot.

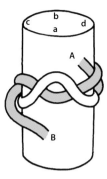

5

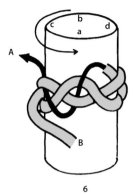

6

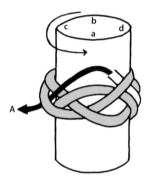

7 Turn the axis slightly clockwise, then tie cord end A backwards according to its original route to make a second layer of knots side by side with the first one.

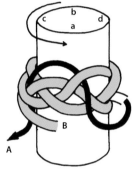

8

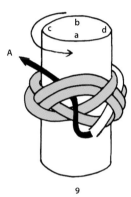

9

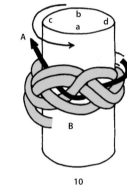

10

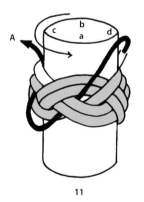

11

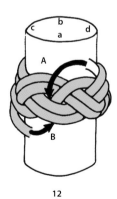

12

13 Completed knot.

Button Ring Knot

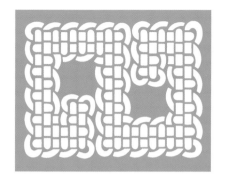

Cloud Formation Knot

This knot is based on the traditional signs for clouds and thunder, hence the name. Clouds, thunder and clouds and thunder together often appeared on ancient copperware and jade pieces in the form of pictographs that the ancient Chinese drew after observing cloud movements and thunder. Later, the motifs simply became decorative designs and were widely used in buildings, fashion and utility items. They are very familiar to the Chinese. The cloud formation knot is an extension of the *pan chang* knot (page 64) with some input from the *bao men* knot (page 70), but here the concept of bending is extended to add further variation.

Tying

The technique is similar to that of the *bao men* knot, except that there are a lot more bends. If a bigger knot is needed, each segment of the knot can be extended proportionately. A series of cloud formation knots is very suitable for decorating the edges of clothing.

Tip

• The tying process puts emphasis on cord end B. Therefore, keep cord end A short and cord end B long.

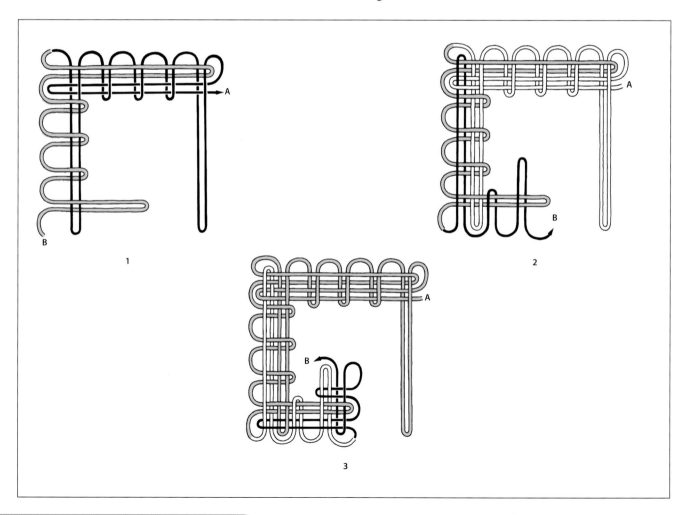

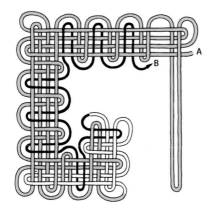

4

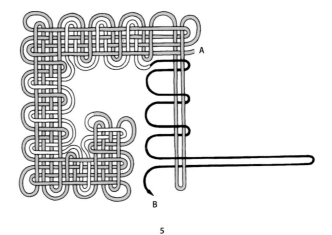

5

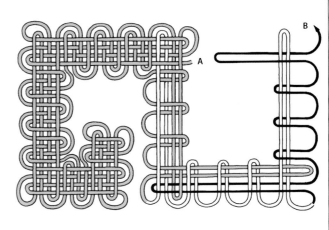

6

7

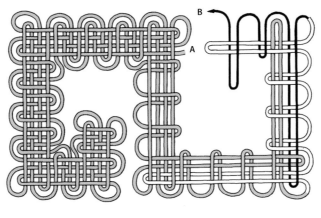

8

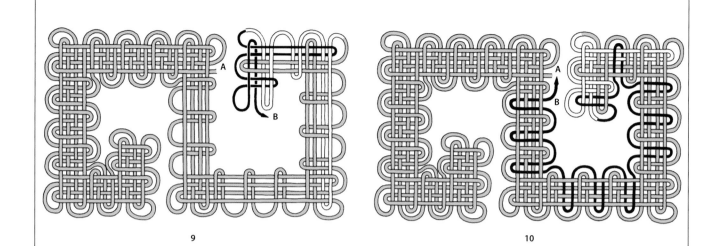

9

10

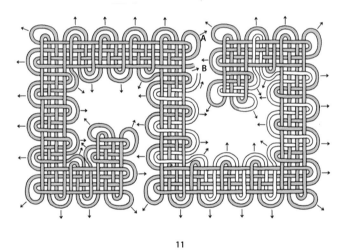

11

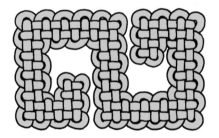

12 Completed knot.

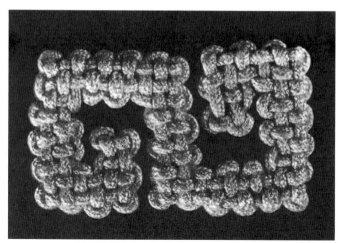

Cloud Formation Knot

Crossed Hui Ling Knot

This is a *hui ling* knot (page 90) with an empty cross-like shape in the center, hence the name. It is formed by extending the body of the knot at the four corners facing the central space. This also serves to strengthen the knot. An ornament can be hung from the center of the knot although it is attractive just by itself.

Tying

Based on the tying technique of the *hui ling* knot, this crossed knot is made by tying further into the inner side of each corner facing the knot center. Upon completion, cord end A will stick out from the knot center while cord end B will remain outside the knot. Cord end A can either be pushed through the body of the knot and used to hang ornaments or other items or both cord ends can be hidden inside the knot body.

Tip

• Keep cord end A longer for tying. If you run short of cord, hook up a new cord with a corner loop or any side loop in order to complete the knot.

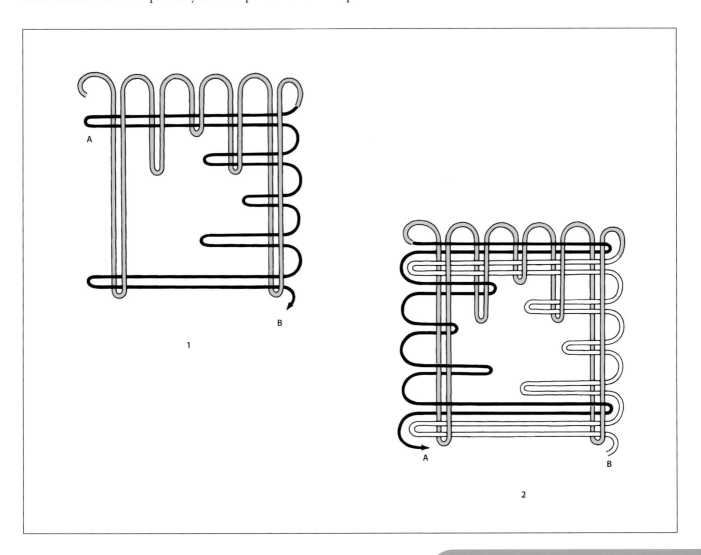

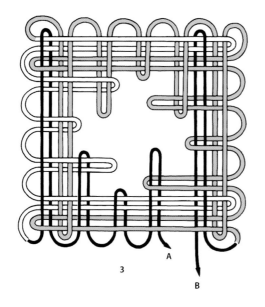

3

A

B

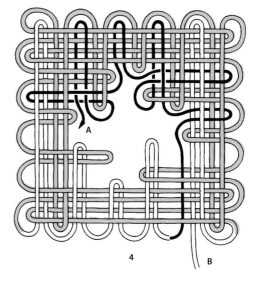

4

A

B

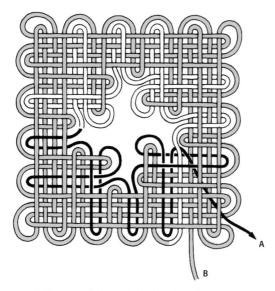

A

B

5 Upon completion of the knot, push cord end A through the body to one corner.

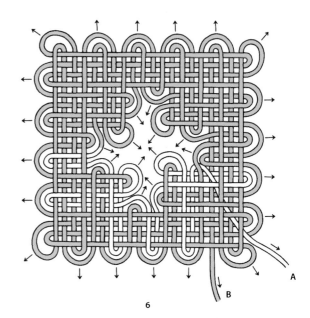

6

A

B

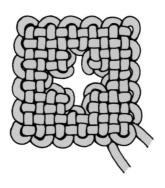

7 Completed knot.

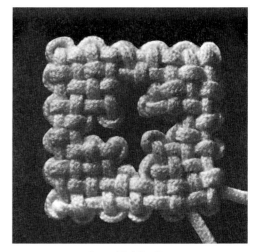

Crossed Hui Ling Knot

Double Hui Ling Knot

This knot comprises two overlapping *hui ling* knots (page 90), hence the "double" in its name. The knot can be hung vertically to decorate a hanging ornament or worn horizontally on a belt.

Tying

First tie a *hui ling* knot. Upon reaching the corner to be overlapped with the second knot, lengthen the pair of outer loops to form the main "trunk" of the second knot. Then carry on completing the first knot. Pull cord end A over the hollow center and through the right side of the overlapped corner to tie the second knot. After completing all the outer loops of the second knot, pull cord end A through the overlapped corner and continue with the second knot.

Tip

• Tighten the cord evenly to ensure that both knots end up identical.

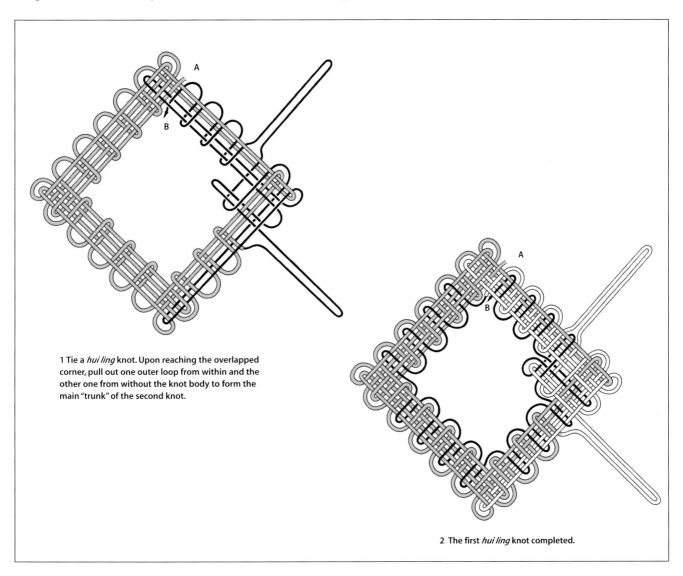

1 Tie a *hui ling* knot. Upon reaching the overlapped corner, pull out one outer loop from within and the other one from without the knot body to form the main "trunk" of the second knot.

2 The first *hui ling* knot completed.

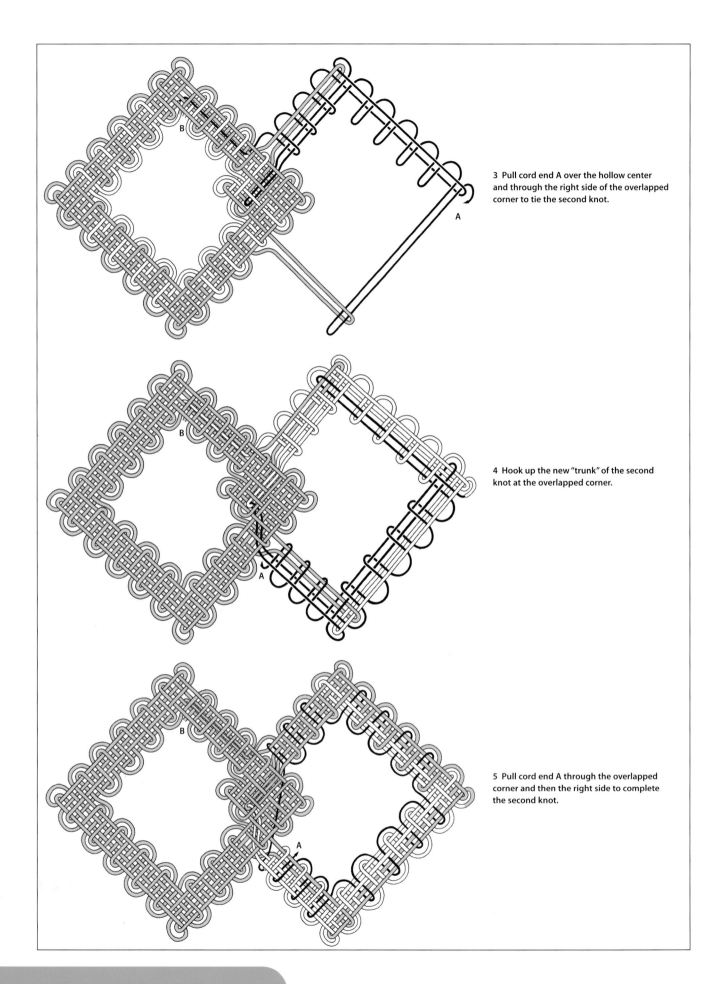

3 Pull cord end A over the hollow center and through the right side of the overlapped corner to tie the second knot.

4 Hook up the new "trunk" of the second knot at the overlapped corner.

5 Pull cord end A through the overlapped corner and then the right side to complete the second knot.

6

7 Completed knot.

Double Hui Ling Knot

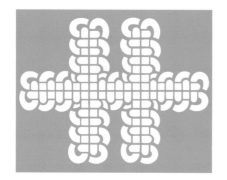

Double Ten Knot

This knot takes the form of two joined crosses, hence the name. It is a simple knot with wide applications. Once familiar with the tying techniques of the knot, it is possible to tie many other knots, such as a simple cross knot (see *Chinese Knotting*, page 45) and a triple ten knot. In addition to being used as a decorative accent on clothing and other items, a series of knots sewn together with fine thread can be used as trimming on clothes and home furnishings.

Tying

Following the tying technique of the *pan chang* knot (page 64), first pull out the main horizontal "trunk," then tie both cord ends into a double cross to complete the knot.

Tip

• During the tightening process, pull slowly and evenly in all four directions to ensure the end product is neat and tidy and not lopsided.

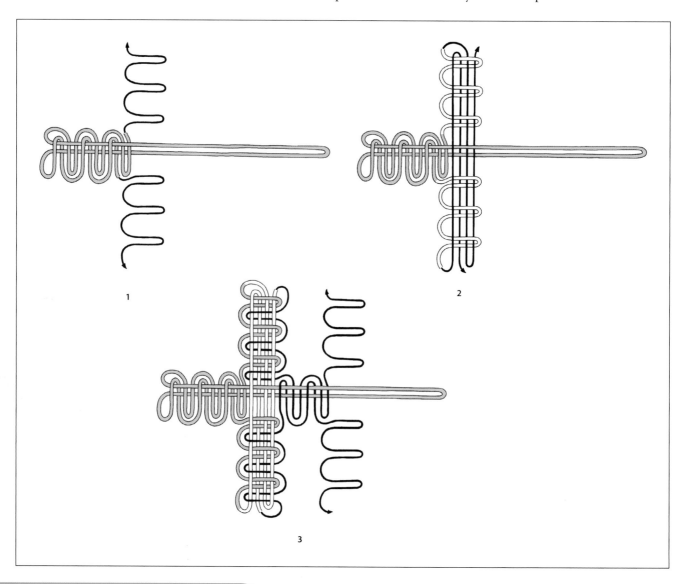

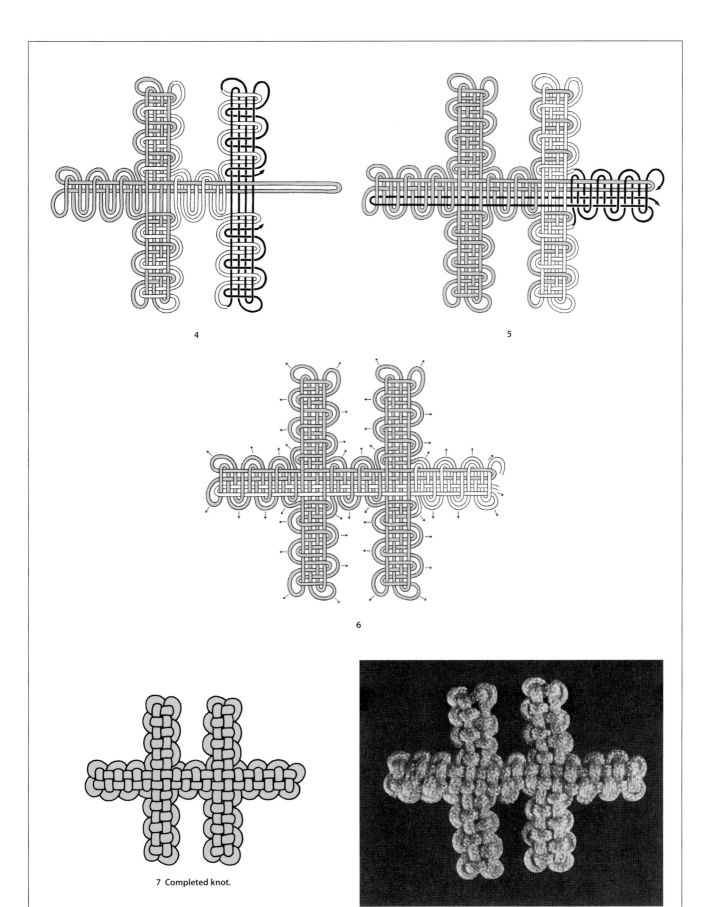

4

5

6

7 Completed knot.

Double Ten Knot

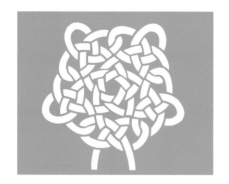

Five Happiness Knot

The early Chinese used the phrase "Cometh forth the five happinesses" to express blessings. According to an ancient script, the five elements of happiness comprise a long life, riches, health, love of virtue and a natural death.

This particular knot derives its name from a flower with five petals. It originates from the ten accord knot (see *Chinese Knotting*, page 86), symbolizing all the things that make up the good things in life, which has a knot body surrounded by four double coin knots. The five happiness knot, however, has five double coin knots as its petals. Since it is a loose structure, it is most suitable as a planar or flat design on garments. If not used in this way, the knot has to be tied with stiff cords and the intersections sewn together.

Tying

In this knot, which is tied using one cord, five double coin knots (page 60) – forming the petals – are hooked up. The center of each knot is formed by intertwining cord from the adjoining double coin knot. Using the same tying technique, new knots with seven or even nine petals can be created, perhaps with names like "Seven Handy …" or "Nine Satisfactory…."

Tips

• When this knot is completed, the cords always overlap in pairs forming a neat one on top one below pattern.
• Make sure that all five double coin knots are identical in terms of shape and size. They must be hooked up snugly to form a tight circle.

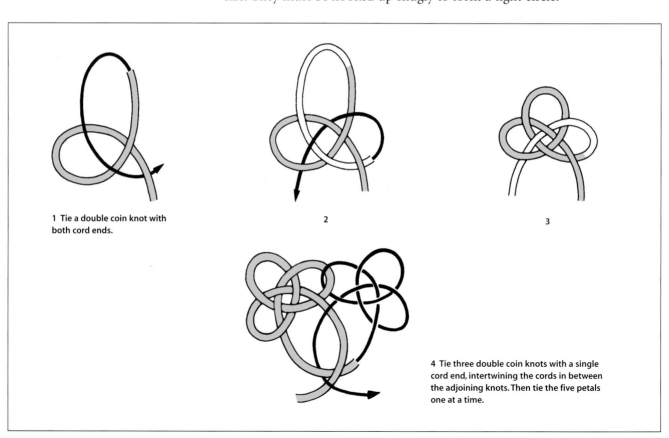

1 Tie a double coin knot with both cord ends.

2

3

4 Tie three double coin knots with a single cord end, intertwining the cords in between the adjoining knots. Then tie the five petals one at a time.

5

6

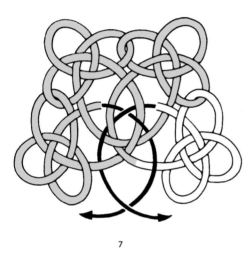

7

8 Complete the five happiness knot by tying a double coin knot at the bottom.

9 Completed knot.

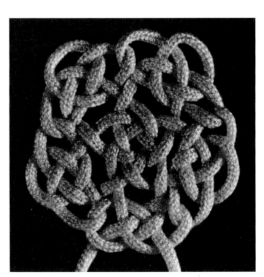

Five Happiness Knot

Golden Bell Knot

This knot is bell-shaped, giving rise to the name golden bell. The knot is tied leaving a bay-like space at the bottom of the *san cai* knot (page 103). The size of the space can be adjusted according to the size of the decorative object to be attached, which can either be chosen to fit completely or partially into the space, according to preference. Alternatively, a tassel can be tied in the space to make a different kind of ornament.

Tying

This knot and the *san cai* knot are both variations of the *pan chang* knot (page 64), except that in this case the two protruding bases are tied separately using two cord ends, thus creating the bay-like space. The size of the knot can be varied to accommodate bigger or smaller objects in the bay.

Tips

• As with the *san cai* knot, anchor each bend to the work surface with push pins to avoid distorting the pattern.
• Use a crochet hook or tweezers to help weave the cord through the pattern.

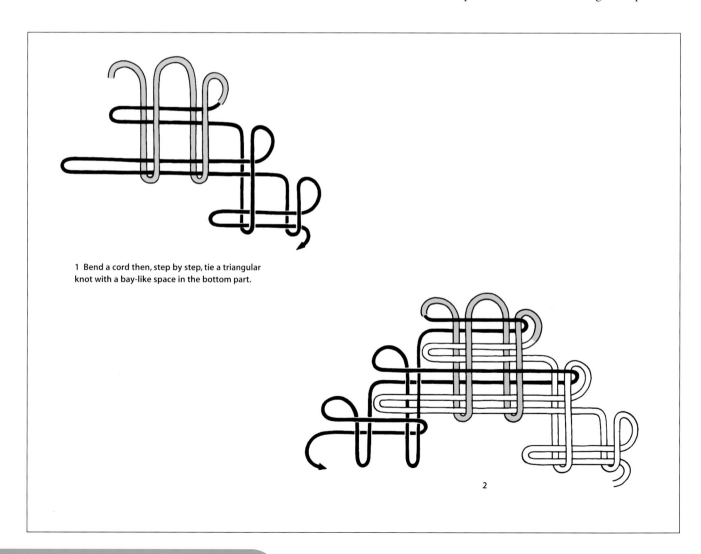

1 Bend a cord then, step by step, tie a triangular knot with a bay-like space in the bottom part.

2

3

4

5

6 Completed knot.

Golden Bell Knot

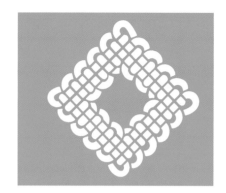

Hui Ling Knot

This is a square knot with a hollow center, hence the name. Basically, the "door space" of the *bao men* knot (page 70) is filled with a *pan chang* knot (page 64) to create a hollow center, in which can be inserted an ornamental object such as a bead or piece of ceramic.

Tying

This knot is an extension of the long *pan chang* knot (see *Chinese Knotting*, page 74). After completing the knot, cord end A can either be hidden inside or pulled through the body of the knot and placed with cord end B on one corner for hanging an ornament, tassel or another knot formation.

Tips

• Make sure cord end A is longer since it is being used for tying.
• For beginners who underestimate the cord length, a new cord can be hooked up with a corner loop or any side loop in order to carry on.

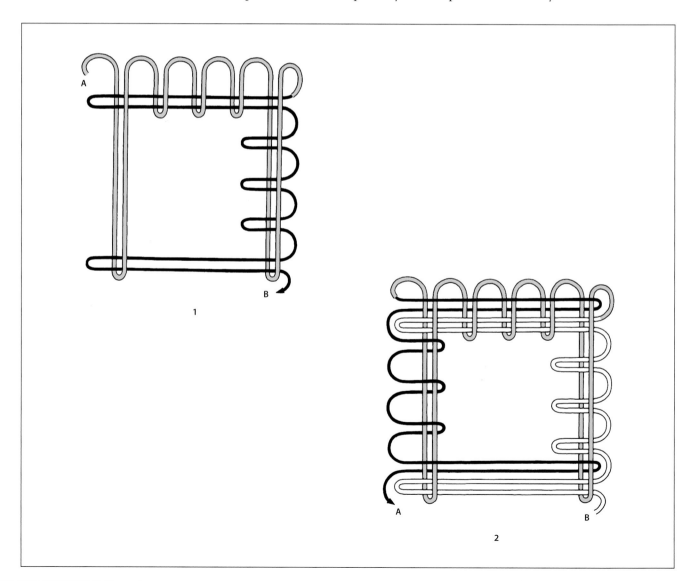

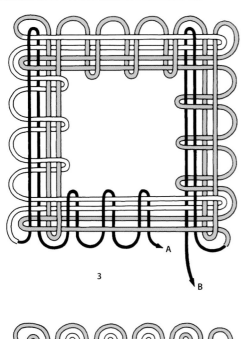

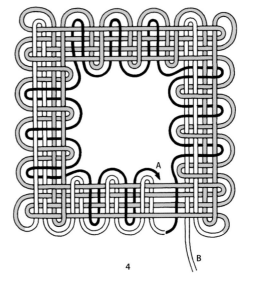

3

4

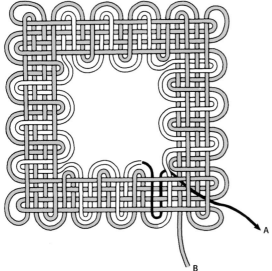

5 After completing the knot, push cord end A through the body of the knot.

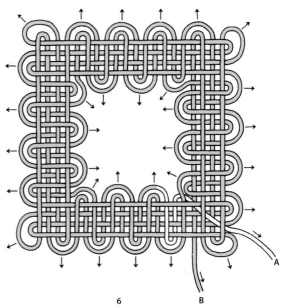

6

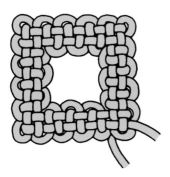

7 Completed knot.

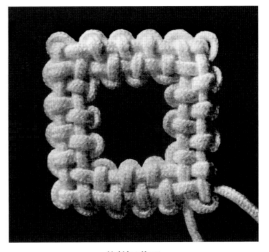

Hui Ling Knot

Ling Hua Knot

This knot resembles a flower called *ling hua* that is frequently depicted on ancient artifacts. It is basically a variation of the *pan chang* knot (page 64), and is akin to two prosperity knots (page 99) joined together. Using this technique, but varying the length and width of the "ladders" around the border, gives rise to a serrated, square or circular *ling hua* knot. Further variations can be created by increasing or decreasing the number of "ladders" around the border.

Tying

Use the tying technique of the prosperity knot to tie the top part of this knot, then use the same technique to complete the bottom half. During the tying process, the width of the "ladders" can be adjusted to form a squarer or more circular knot, and hence a taller or shorter knot. The outer loops can be lengthened and twisted to form other designs.

Tip

• During the tightening process, pull the cord slowly and evenly on all sides to avoid distorting the shape.

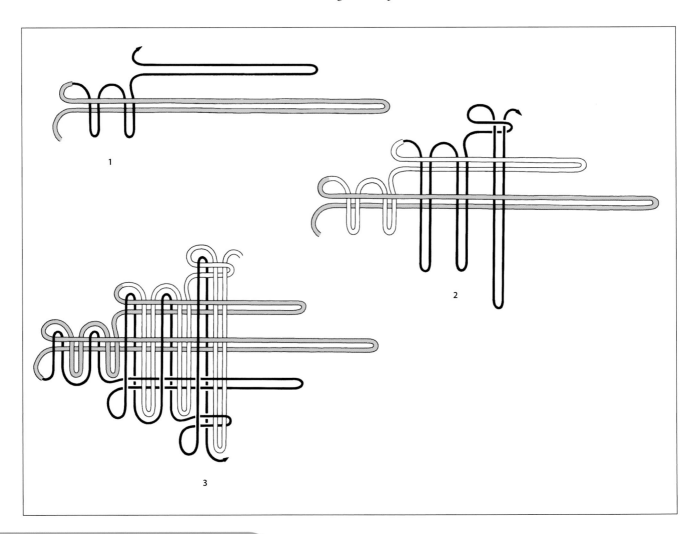

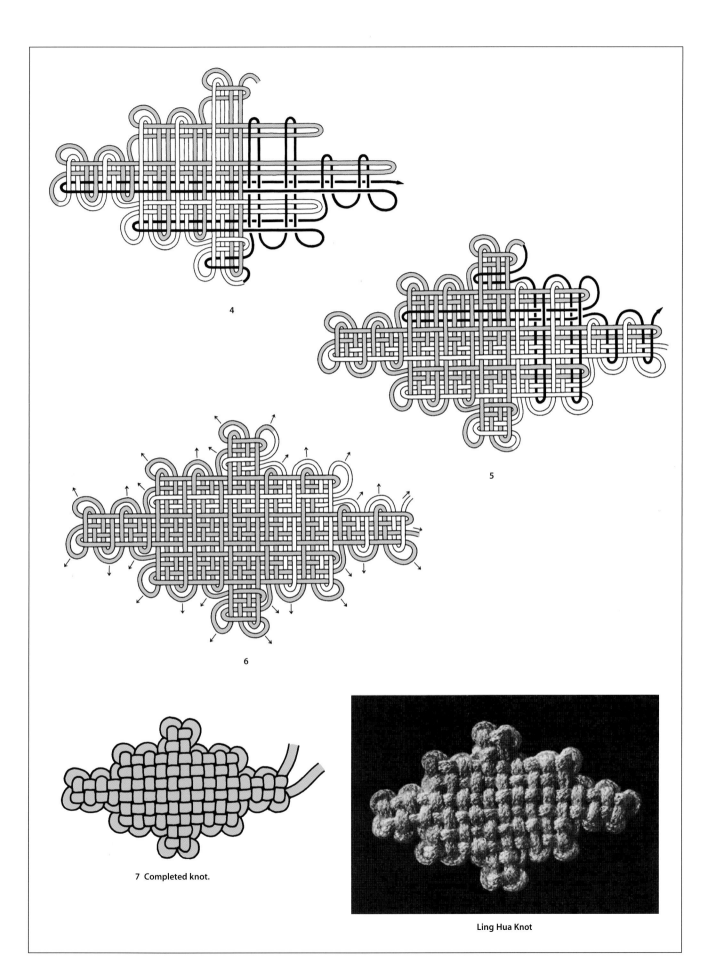

4

5

6

7 Completed knot.

Ling Hua Knot

Love Knot

While both the double *hui ling* knot (page 90) and the love knot comprise two overlapping *hui ling* knots, in the love knot the two *hui ling* knots overlap at the hollow centers or the "heart" of the knot, hence the name.

Tying

First tie a *hui ling* knot. Upon reaching the overlap, pull out the two outer loops to form the main "trunk" of the second *hui ling* knot. Then complete the first knot and tie the corner of the second knot that resides within the first one. Pull cord end A through the overlapped side on the right-hand side and carry on making the second knot.

Tips

• Make sure both knots are tightened to identical sizes. Tighten sequentially until you reach the bend within the right overlap, then hold it down with a few lightly sewn stitches, and then carry on tightening.
• Pull the cords at each overlap as straight as possible and hold them down with stitches.

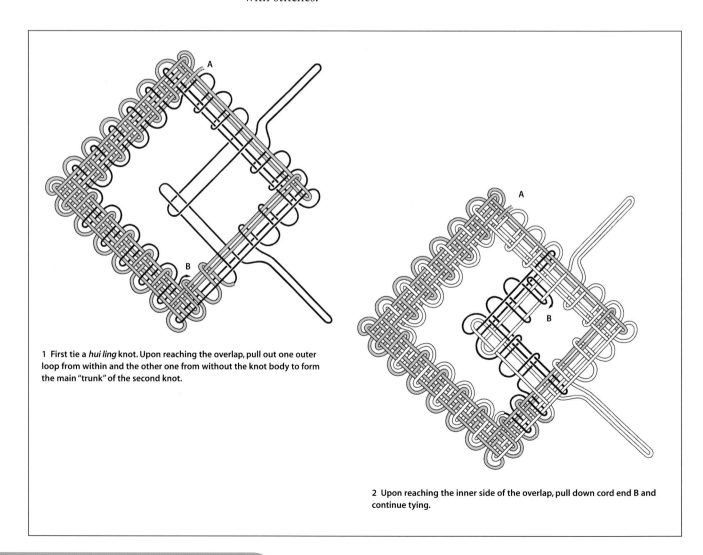

1 First tie a *hui ling* knot. Upon reaching the overlap, pull out one outer loop from within and the other one from without the knot body to form the main "trunk" of the second knot.

2 Upon reaching the inner side of the overlap, pull down cord end B and continue tying.

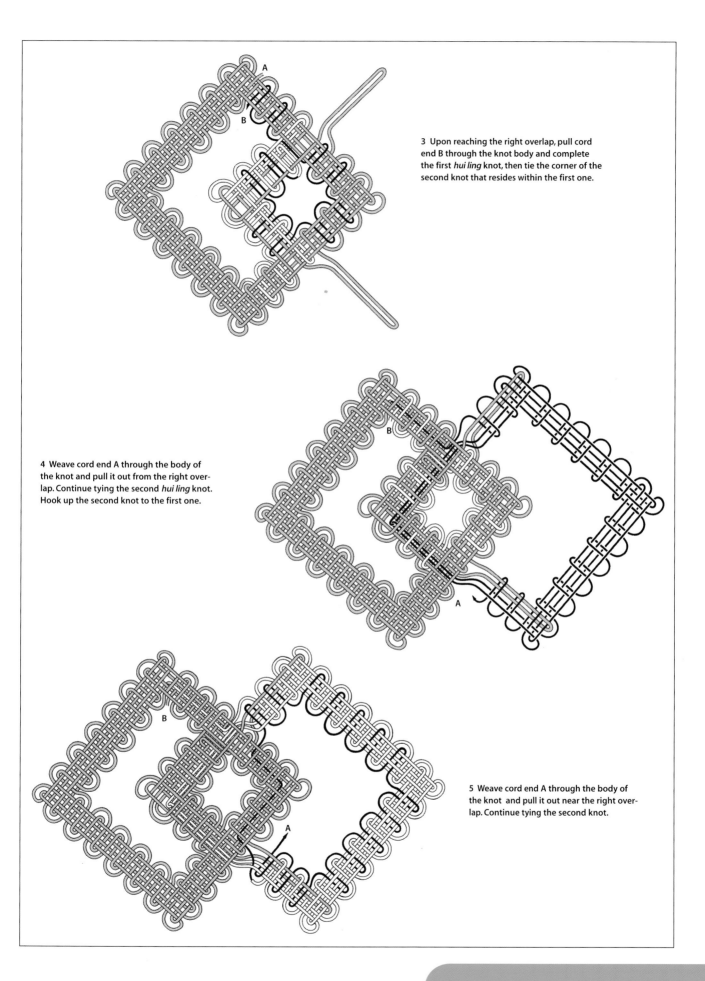

3 Upon reaching the right overlap, pull cord end B through the knot body and complete the first *hui ling* knot, then tie the corner of the second knot that resides within the first one.

4 Weave cord end A through the body of the knot and pull it out from the right overlap. Continue tying the second *hui ling* knot. Hook up the second knot to the first one.

5 Weave cord end A through the body of the knot and pull it out near the right overlap. Continue tying the second knot.

6

7 Completed knot.

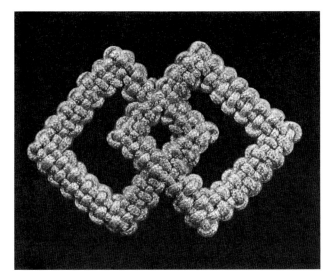

Love Knot

Multiple Winged Pan Chang Knot

This is another variation on the *pan chang* knot (page 64). It has multiple overlapping wings on all sides, hence its name. Wings like these can be added to all *pan chang* knot variations, such as the *san cai* knot (page 103).

Tying

Change the tying sequence of the *pan chang* knot to create the multiple wing effect.

Tips

• Though using the same technique, the shape of the knot can change due to the different sizes of the wings.
• Hold the center of the knot firmly so that it does not loosen before and during adjustment of the wings.

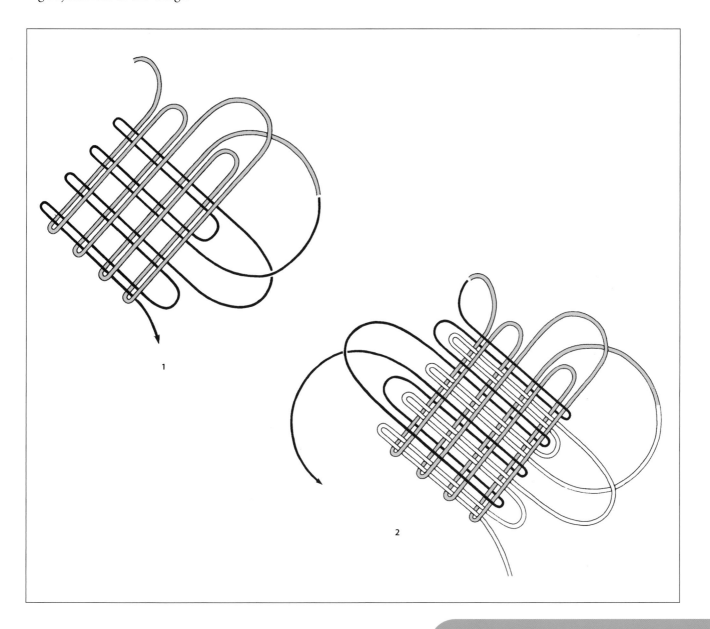

3

4

5 Completed knot.

Multiple Winged Pan Chang Knot

Prosperity Knot

"Keep prospering" is a traditional greeting among the Chinese. This knot is ladder-shaped, denoting prosperity, hence the name. It is a variation of the *san cai* knot (page 103), ascending into a taller ladder.

Tying

The tying technique here is similar to that of the *san cai* knot. The step of the ladder can be lengthened to suit individual preferences. However, the height of the step must take up at least two outer loops or otherwise it will become a *san cai* knot.

Tips

• Anchor the bends with push pins to avoid distorting the pattern.
• Use a crochet hook or tweezers to help weave the cord through the pattern.

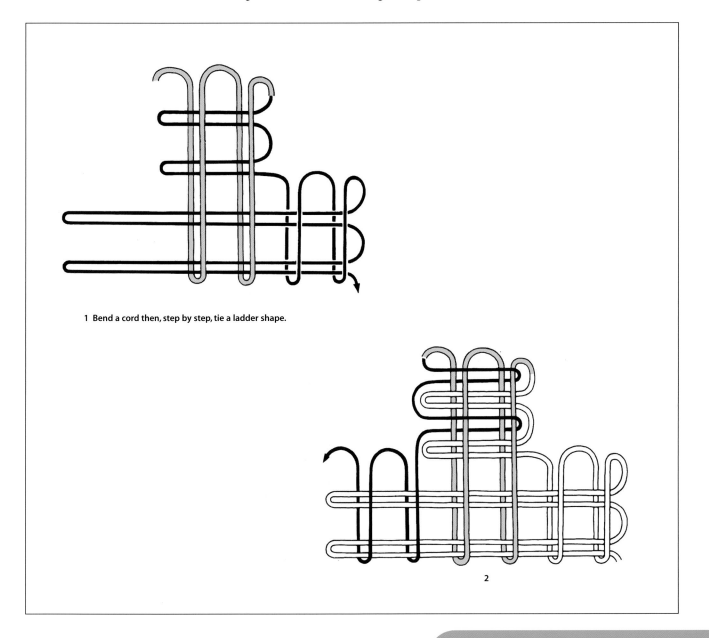

1 Bend a cord then, step by step, tie a ladder shape.

2

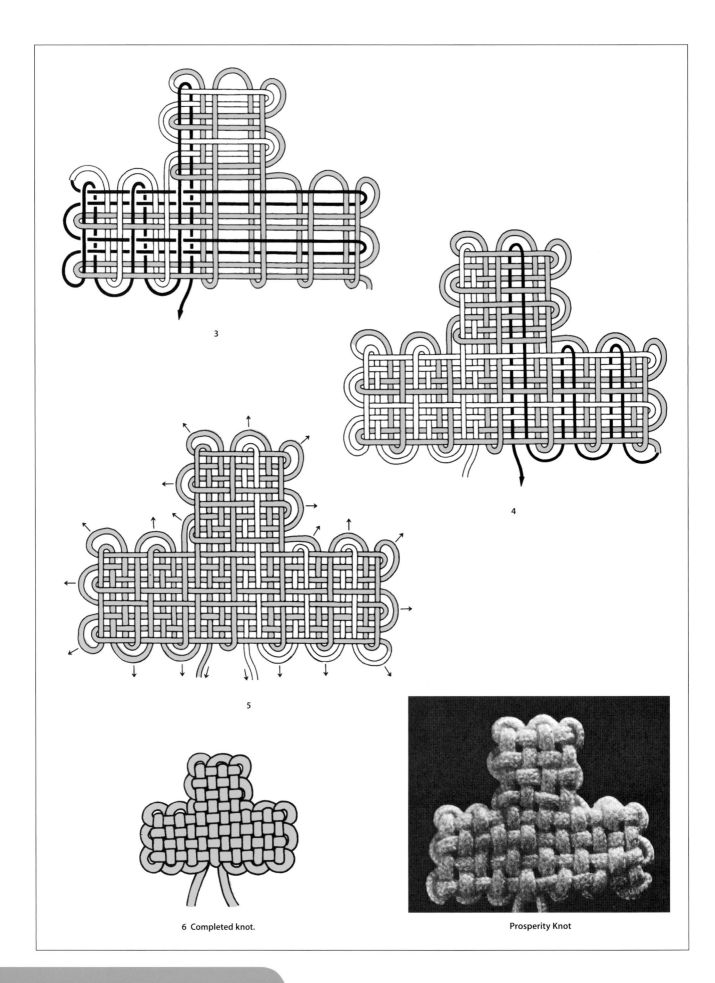

3

4

5

6 Completed knot.

Prosperity Knot

Ru Yi Knot

The *ru yi* is an elongated scepter about the length of a back scratcher. Its two rounded ends are flattened and scalloped, and this is echoed in this knot. The name *ru yi* means "everything according to your heart's desire." Some say that the *ru yi* scepter came to China with early Buddhist missionaries, who used a similar-shaped device as a note-taking surface during explications of the sutras. Others assert that the *ru yi* is indigenous in origin, pointing to the fact that its rounded ends are strikingly similar to a Taoist motif signifying immortality. Whatever its origins, the *ru yi* is a symbol of great fortune. To carry one is to court good luck, and to own one is to enjoy prosperity.

Tying

The *ru yi* is made up of four cloverleaf knots (page 57), the one in the center bringing the three outer ones together. First, tie three cloverleaf knots in a series on one cord, several centimeters apart. Then use the two loops that hang down between them and the two loose cord ends to tie a fourth cloverleaf, the loops of which will run directly into the bodies of the outer knots. Adjust and tighten so that the loops of all four knots are the same size.

Tips

• Remember not to let the centers of the cloverleaf knots loosen when you are taking out slack. Hold the bodies firmly while running the extra cord through.
• The diagrams show how to tie the *ru yi* knot using both ends of the cord. Eventually, some formations will require you to tie it using only one end. This will mean tying one of the outer cloverleaf knots first, instead of the top one, and tying the center one in stages as you proceed from one outer knot to the top one to the other outer knot.

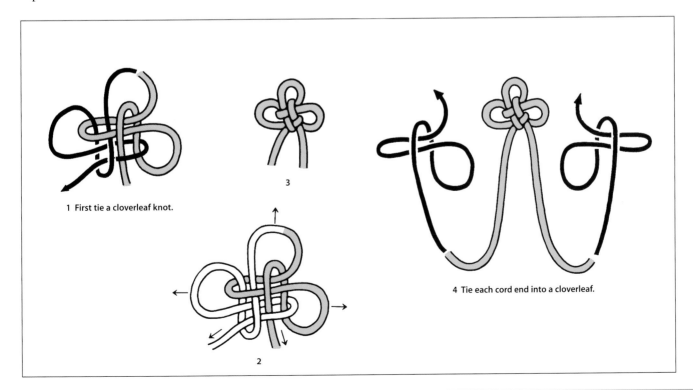

1 First tie a cloverleaf knot.

3

2

4 Tie each cord end into a cloverleaf.

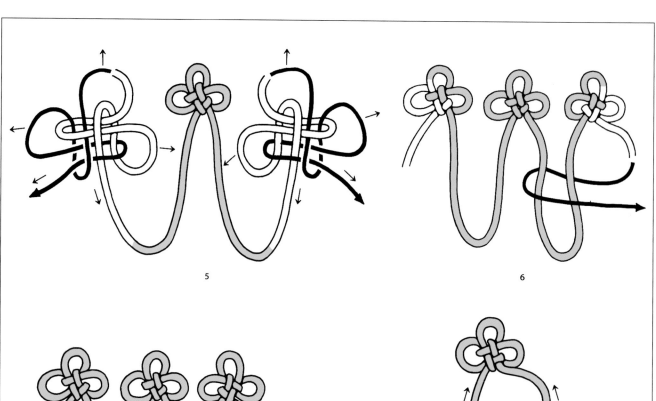

5

6

7 Use the sections of cord connecting the three knots and both cord ends to tie another cloverleaf knot.

8

9 Completed knot.

Ru Yi Knot

San Cai Knot

This knot has three corners representing the sky, the earth and human beings, hence the name *san cai*. The knot derives from the long *pan chang* or mystic knot (see *Chinese Knotting*, page 74), one of the eight Buddhist treasures, but the method of bending the cord is different.

Tying

Use a single cord to tie this knot. Depending on the form of the triangle desired, bend the cords in the long *pan chang* knot at different lengths. If you wish to make an equilateral triangle during the tying process, extend the "ladder" downward. On completion of the knot, the cord ends should appear at the bottom of the knot. If the cord ends are pushed through the top part of the knot, the whole knot can be inverted.

Tips

• Anchor every bend to the work surface with a push pin, making sure that the proportions are correct.
• Use a crochet hook or tweezers to help weave the cord through the pattern.

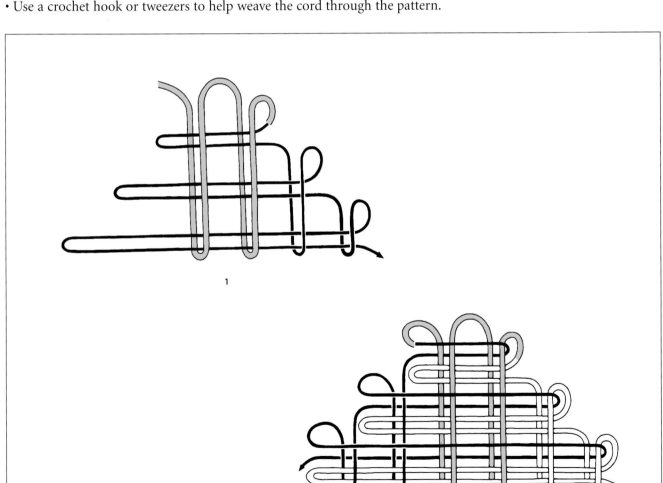

1

2

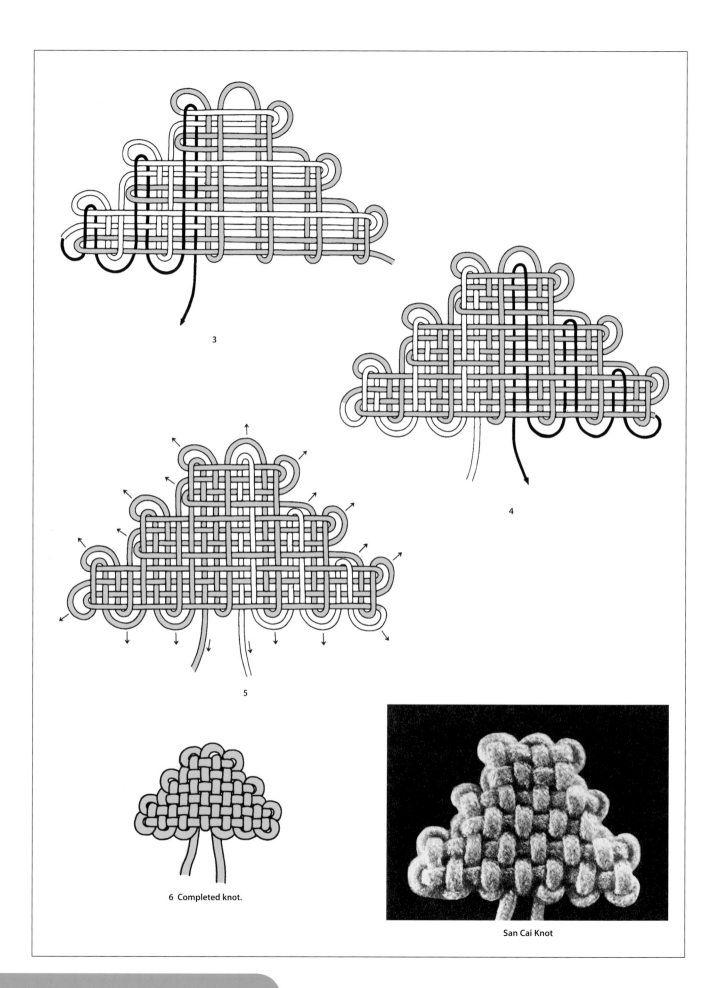

3

4

5

6 Completed knot.

San Cai Knot

Six Unity Knot

The sky, the earth and the four directions of north, east, south and west form the six components of unity. Since ancient times, the Chinese have used the phrase "The six unity in springtime" to denote that everything on earth prospers in spring. This knot, with its six petals, originates from the ten accord knot (see *Chinese Knotting*, page 86), hence the name six unity.

Tying

This knot, made from a single cord, is similar to the five happiness knot (page 86) except that it has six hooked-up double coin knots instead of five. Using the same tying technique, other compound knots with an even number of knots, such as eight or ten, can form the petals. Since the knot goes out of shape easily, it is advisable to tie it with stiff cords and sew the intersections.

Tips

• When the knot is completed, the cords should overlap in pairs, with a neat one-on-top one-below pattern.
• Make sure that all six double coin knots are identical and are hooked up snugly to form a tight circle.

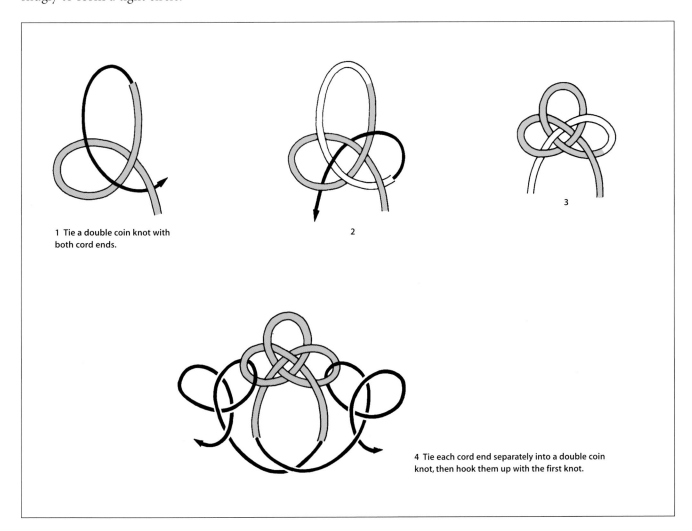

1 Tie a double coin knot with both cord ends.

2

3

4 Tie each cord end separately into a double coin knot, then hook them up with the first knot.

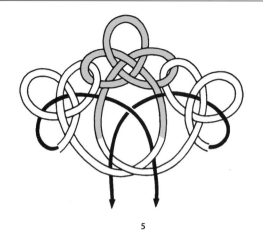

5

6 The cords in between the two cord ends and the double coin knots must be intertwined. Then tie another two double coin knots.

7 Weave the cord ends to make the six-petal design in the center.

8 Complete the six unity knot by tying a final double coin knot at the bottom.

9 Completed knot.

Six Unity Knot

Stone Chime Knot

The stone chime is an ancient Chinese percussion instrument made with an L-shaped piece of sonorous stone or jade. Composed of a series of stones, graduated according to size and thickness, it is often hung from a two-tiered wooden rack. Used in ritual orchestral ensembles, the stone chime is struck with a mallet, its crisp tone marking the end of a musical phrase. Stone chimes are indispensable in Confucian music, which is noted for its grandeur and symbolism. Musical performance in this tradition is an expression of social ethics. The music of the sage-ruler deeply moves his listeners, the people, steering them towards righteousness and creating lasting peace under under the heavens.

Tying

The stone chime knot is made up of two long *pan chang* knots (see *Chinese Knotting*, page 74) woven together at right angles, sharing a common corner. The warp and weft of each *pan chang* can be increased to make a larger stone chime knot. The weaving pattern is the same as in any *pan chang* variation.

Tip

• The only problem likely to be encountered is the tightening. Tighten one long *pan chang* completely first. Then watch out for distortion in the shared corner when you tighten the other one.

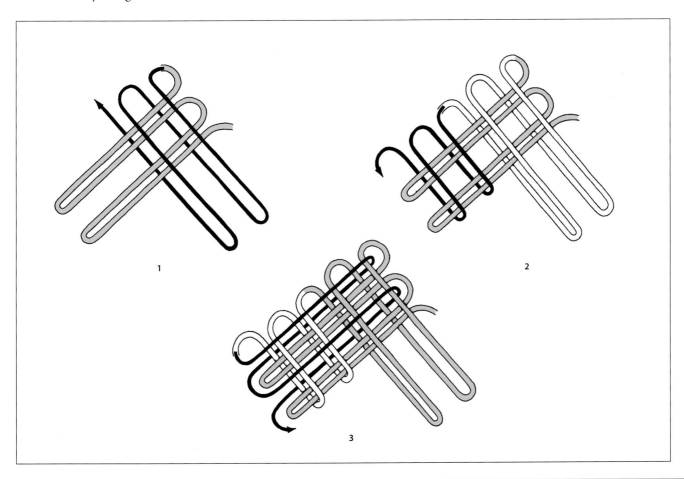

1

2

3

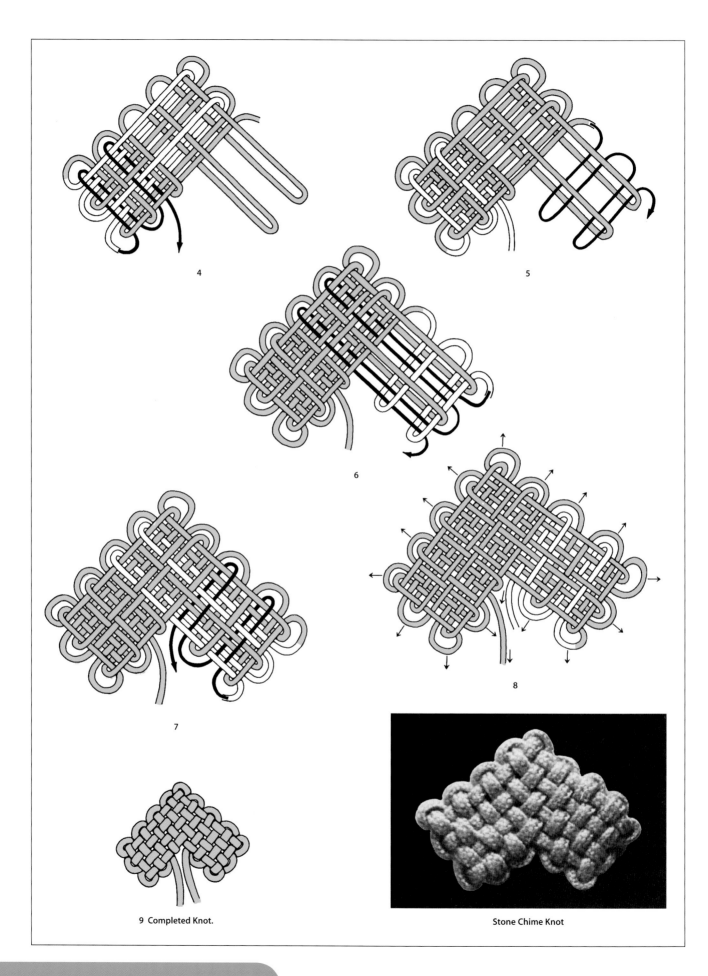

4

5

6

7

8

9 Completed Knot.

Stone Chime Knot

Winged Pan Chang Knot

This is a modified *pan chang* knot (page 64), with each outer loop bearing three heart shapes, hence the name. Such shapes can be added to all *pan chang* knot variations, such as the *san cai* knot (page 103).

Tying

Change the tying sequence of the *pan chang* knot to create the three heart shapes in the outer loops. More heart shapes can be added to an outer loop by increasing its size.

Tips

• Adjust the size of each heart shape to highlight this knot.
• Hold down the body of the knot before and during adjustment of the heart shapes.

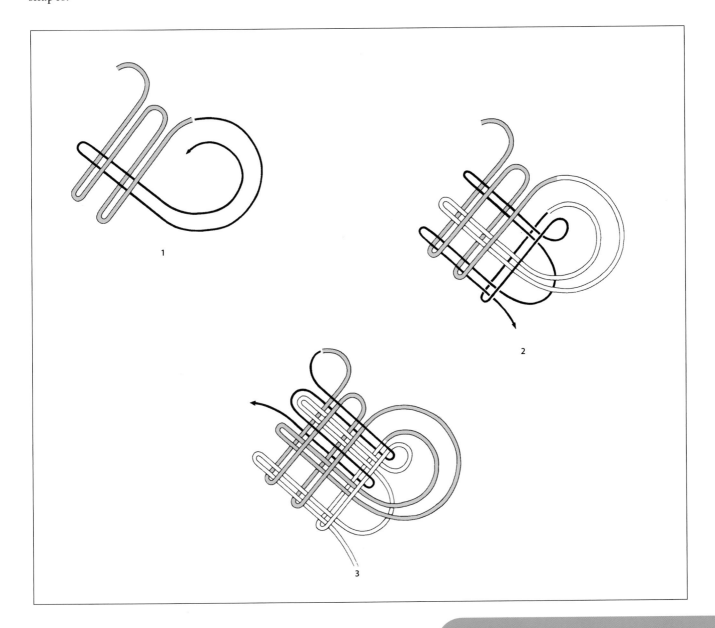

1

2

3

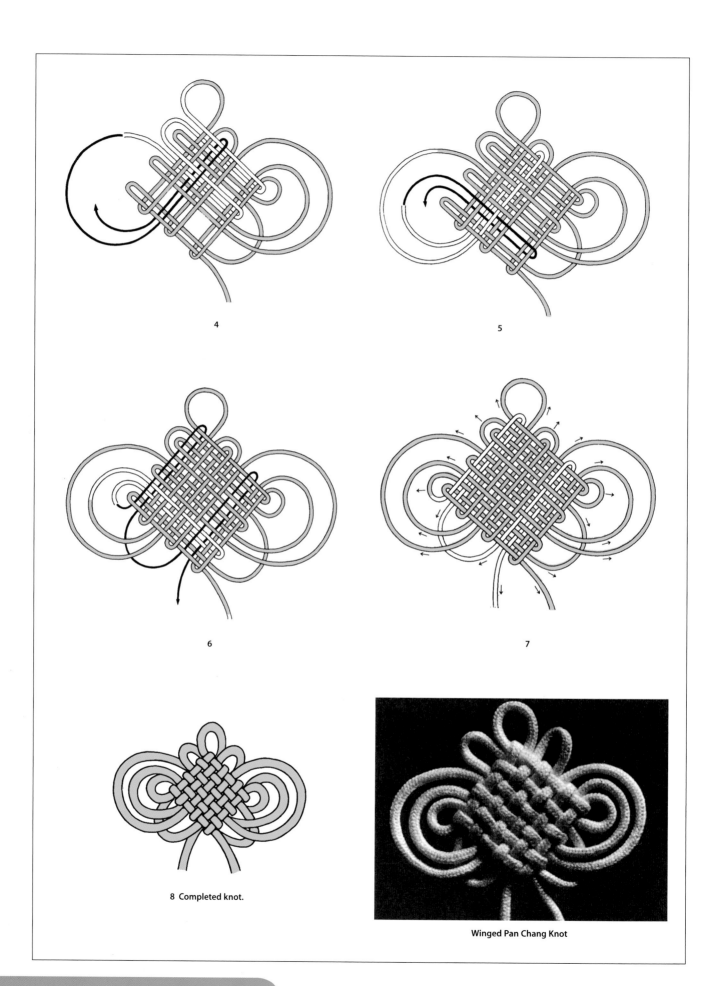

4

5

6

7

8 Completed knot.

Winged Pan Chang Knot

Tassel Designs

A tassel is a hanging ornament comprising a stiff head at the top and a bundle of soft cords at the bottom. Adding an appropriate tassel to an object or to a knot formation can greatly enhance its beauty.

Tassels used to be commonplace in the daily lives of many Chinese, and are still frequently found hanging from lanterns, bed mosquito nets, bed canopies, wall hangings and other household objects, adding a touch of gaiety and "Chineseness." They were also commonly attached to the ends of smaller personal items, such as fans, spectacle cases, bags, pouches and pendants.

In this section, instructions for making five common tassels – the love tassel, button tassel, good luck tassel, horizontal weave tassel and diagonal weave tassel – are given.

The techniques for tying tassels are not, of course, limited to these five types. For example, there is one particular technique where the tassel head is made from a thick cord formed from a bundle of thinner cords. With this type of cord, the fine cords can be unraveled to produce two tassels at both ends. A slightly different type of tassel can also be made by tying the remaining cord ends of a knot formation into a double coin knot, cloverleaf knot or other knot and inserting beads. With imagination and improvisation, any number of other tassels can be devised for adorning clothes, accessories, ornaments and home furnishings.

Button Tassel

This tassel has a head formed from a button knot (page 55), hence its name.

Tying

A button tassel is usually made by first tying a button knot using the remaining cord ends of a knot formation and then fixing this head to some tassel cords made from the same or different materials as the tassel head. Alternatively, the button tassel can be tied first and the remaining cord ends of a knot formation then sewn into the head.

If a stiffer tassel head is required, the button knot can be tied simultaneously with two or more cords, although this tends to produce tangles. It is best to tie a double-layer knot with a single cord by first tying a button knot without tightening it, and then sewing the two cord ends together just below the head, and finally using the cord ends to follow the weave separately in the reverse direction. If a two-color button tassel is required, a second cord can be used to tie a second layer following the same weave of the first. If more cords are preferred, one or more cords can be folded and sewn into the tassel knot.

Tip

• A two-layer and two-color button tassel has the advantages of having a bigger head with a more pronounced weave.

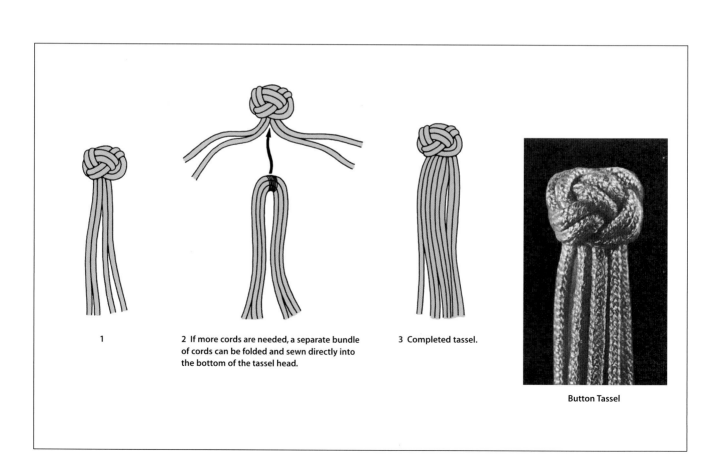

1

2 **If more cords are needed, a separate bundle of cords can be folded and sewn directly into the bottom of the tassel head.**

3 **Completed tassel.**

Button Tassel

Diagonal Weave Tassel

As with the love knot (page 96), the head and cords of this tassel originate from the same center. However, the technique employed is more like that of the horizontal weave tassel (page 116), except that the latitudinal cord is woven diagonally downward to form the tassel head.

Tying

Fold a bundle of cords and tie the bend with a thread. Pull the thread through the hole of a bead until the bundle of cords and the bead are close together. Invert the bead and arrange the cord tassels so that they cover the bead evenly. Fasten the cords tightly just below the bead either with the thread protruding from the bead or with a new thread. This completes the love tassel. Invert the bead again. Treating the cords covering the bead as the longitudinal ones and the hanging cords as the latitudinal ones, pull down each latitudinal cord in turn and thread it downward through its corresponding longitudinal cord. Using a method similar to weaving cloth, pull each latitudinal cord in turn across the first neighboring longitudinal one on the right and weave it into the second neighboring longitudinal cord until all the latitudinal cords are done. If you wish to narrow the gaps between the hanging tassel cords, fold another thread and sew it into the base just below the head. Finally, hook the remaining cord ends of the already completed knot formation into the tassel head with a crochet hook and sew in place.

To make a two-color diagonal weave tassel, wrap cords of two different colors covered with strong glue around the hollow bead, employing the same technique used for the horizontal weave tassel. Then, fasten the cords just below the bead with a thread and arrange the cords neatly. Finally, weave each latitudinal cord according to the technique described above. To make a tassel with three colors or more, simply extend the procedure.

Tips

• Use oblong beads or cylinders instead of round beads for variety.
• The nearer you end the weaving of the latitudinal cords to the center of the bead base, the denser the tassel cords become. To achieve the intended tassel cord density, you can decide the exact place to end the weaving process.

1

2

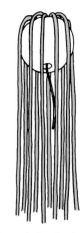

3 Invert the bead and arrange the cords neatly around it.

4 Use the thread protruding from the bead to fasten the tassel cords just below the bead.

5

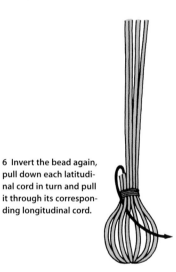

6 Invert the bead again, pull down each latitudinal cord in turn and pull it through its corresponding longitudinal cord.

7 Pull each latitudinal cord in turn downward across the first neighboring longitudinal cord on the right and weave it into the second neighboring longitudinal cord.

8 Completed tassel.

Diagonal Weave Tassel

Good Luck Tassel

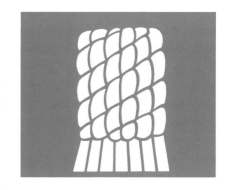

This tassel comprises a cylindrical head and tassel cords. Its tying method is very similar to that of the good luck knot (page 62), from which it gets its name.

Tying

Cross two cords at their centers. Following the tying method of the good luck knot, fold one cord on top of the other one, as shown in step 2, and tighten to make the first layer, as in step 3. Repeat this folding and tightening sequence on the bottom side of the knot to make a second layer. Continue the sequence until you reach the required head length, then secure the four cord ends with a needle and thread. For a bigger tassel head, tie two or more cords as one. If need be, fold and sew another bundle of cords into the bottom part of the head (see step 2, page 112). Finally, hook the cord ends of the completed knot formation to the tassel head with a crochet hook and stitch in place.

Tips

• There are two sequential folding techniques. One is to fold each layer sequentially clockwise, while the other is to alternately fold clockwise and counter-clockwise for the different layers. The former results in a cylindrical tassel head with a slanting grain, while the latter produces a cube with a straight grain. Do not mix the techniques in the same tassel head.
• Use different colored cords to add interest to the tassel.

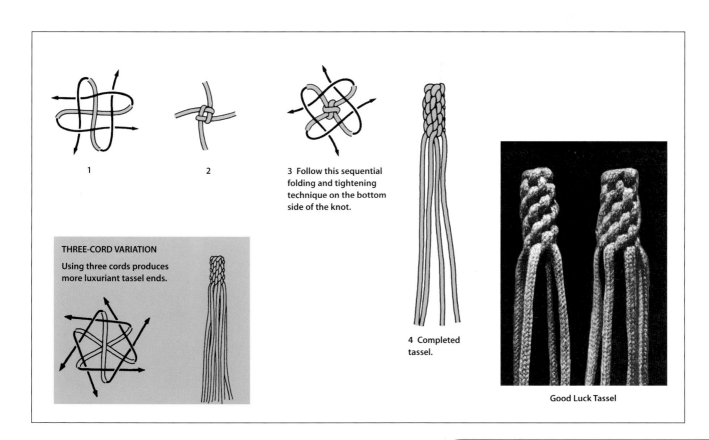

1

2

3 Follow this sequential folding and tightening technique on the bottom side of the knot.

THREE-CORD VARIATION

Using three cords produces more luxuriant tassel ends.

4 Completed tassel.

Good Luck Tassel

Horizontal Weave Tassel

This tassel has a head tied with longitudinal and latitudinal cords. The longitudinal cords are fixed in position, but the latitudinal cords can be inserted in a variety of ways to produce different results.

Tying

Fold an odd number of cords to make the longitudinal cords and wrap them around a cylinder. After the cylinder is covered, start weaving the latitudinal threads, one by one in and out of the longitudinal cords, then sew each end into the tassel head. Finally, hook the cord ends of the already completed knot formation into the tassel head with a crochet hook and sew in place.

Tips

• After tying each longitudinal cord to the cylinder, fasten it at the bottom of the cylinder with a thread to keep it taut, then only start weaving in the latitudinal cords.
• Irregular weaving of the latitudinal cord will create different patterns or even "words of good luck" on the tassel head.

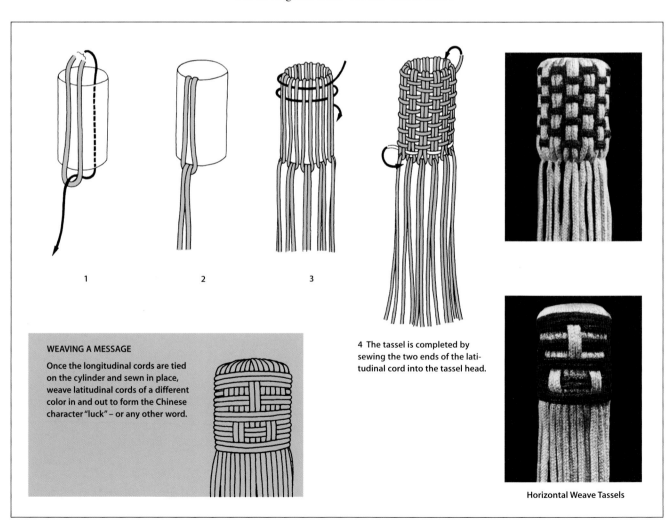

1   2   3

WEAVING A MESSAGE
Once the longitudinal cords are tied on the cylinder and sewn in place, weave latitudinal cords of a different color in and out to form the Chinese character "luck" – or any other word.

4 The tassel is completed by sewing the two ends of the latitudinal cord into the tassel head.

Horizontal Weave Tassels

Love Tassel

In this tassel, the head and cords all originate from one center, hence the connotation of "love." All that is required is to fasten, invert and refasten a bundle of cords.

Tying

Fold a bundle of cords in half and fasten them at the bend with a thread, then smooth out any tangles. At a suitable distance from the first thread, tie a second one to form the tassel head. Invert the tassel head so that it is covered by the cords, then fasten the cords with a third thread. If a bigger head is required, try fastening, inverting and retying the cords until the desired size is reached. The head can also be made firmer or bigger with cotton, cloth, paper or a ball-like object. To attach the tassel to an already completed knot formation, insert the cord ends of the knot formation into the tassel head with a crochet hook and sew in place.

Tips

• Tidy the tassel cords before every step to avoid entanglement.
• Make sure that each tassel cord falls evenly from the center so that the tassel head is completely and evenly covered.

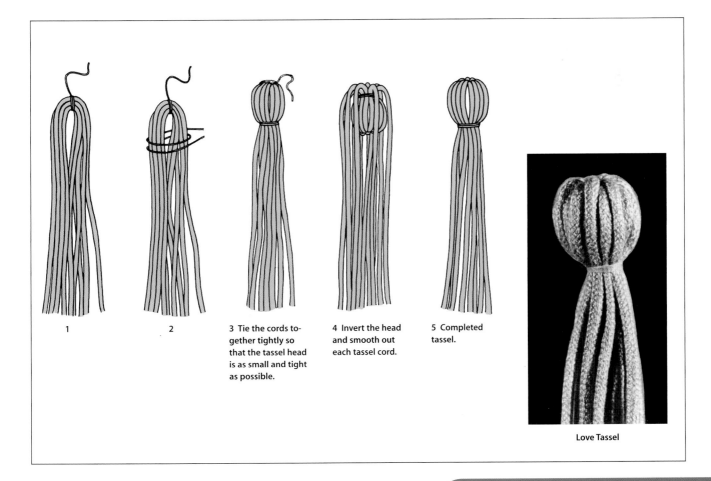

1

2

3 Tie the cords together tightly so that the tassel head is as small and tight as possible.

4 Invert the head and smooth out each tassel cord.

5 Completed tassel.

Love Tassel

Creative Applications

In this chapter, detailed notes and diagrams are given for 135 knotting applications: 1–123 are illustrated in the color photographs in "Living With Chinese Knots" (pages 27–54) and 124–135 in "Designing Chinese Knots" (pages 8–26). It is important to note the following, with reference to the diagrams on page 119:

• Finished knot formations may differ a little from those shown on pages 27–54 because everyone knots in a slightly different way. However, the tying of the basic and compound knots does not change. Read "Designing Chinese Knots" (pages 8–26) carefully before attempting to tie any of the knot formations in this chapter and keep referring to it as you follow the instructions.

• The description of each knot formation starts with the first knot and proceeds step by step to the last knot in the formation. The numbers on the diagrams generally indicate the order in which each knot is completed. For example, in diagram A, the *ru yi, pan chang* and button knots are completed in the order 1, 2, 3. But things are a little different in diagram B because a knot that is tied first does not necessarily mean it will be completed first. The central round brocade knot is the first to be tied, but it is not the first to be completed because a cloverleaf knot has to be tied on the outer loop on each side first before going back to the round brocade knot. Hence, the central round brocade knot becomes knot number 3 in the diagram. Another example is given in diagram C. Although the stone chime and round brocade knots on both sides are tied first, they are not tightened immediately. Another cord has to be introduced into the stone chime knot and woven in the reverse order before being extended into a series of cloverleaf knots, after which both cords are tightened. Thus, even though the stone chime knot is the second knot to be tied, it is numbered 12 in the diagram. In the case of complicated knot formations like these, it is important to refer closely to both the written description and the numbered diagrams.

• When making a knot formation consisting of compound or extension knots, we normally follow the example shown in diagram B of tying the right side of the knot formation first, followed by the left side. Similarly, in the tying process we normally follow the directional words given, such as "top," "bottom," "left part," "right part," "left cord end," "right cord end." But this does not necessarily reflect how the completed formation will be used. Take the knot button in diagram D as an example. When applied to clothing, this formation is placed horizontally. However, during the tying process, knots 1–3 actually form the right part and knots 4–6 the left part of the button. Diagram E is another example. At a glance, most people would think that the knot formation was tied from the bottom upwards. In actual fact, knot 1 is the top part of the formation and the butterfly (20) and the cloverleaf knots (21, 22) the bottom part, since we need to use the cord ends to decorate the top part of the evening gown.

• When a long formation is made using several knots of the same type, the knot is usually indicated with a single number. For example, in diagram F only one number is used to indicate all the double coin knots even though the number of knots tied can be reduced or increased to suit one's needs.

• Each number in a diagram indicates a complete knot. Hence, all rim embellishments, whether in or around the knot, are not given numbers. For example, upon the completion of the *pan chang* knot (1) in diagram G, one of the cord ends is used to embellish the rim before the winged *pan chang* knot is tied. Here the rim embellishment is not numbered.

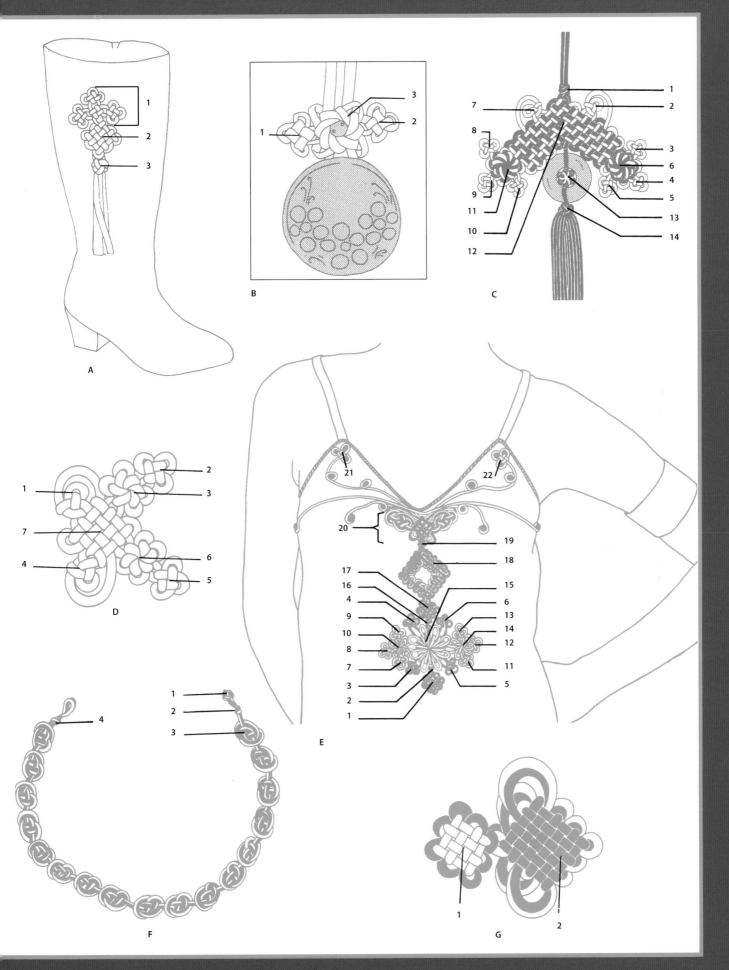

HAIR ORNAMENTS

See pages 28–29 for photographs of applications 1–14.

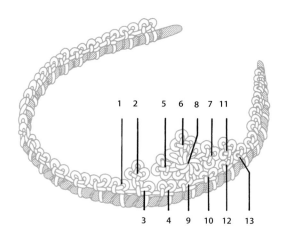

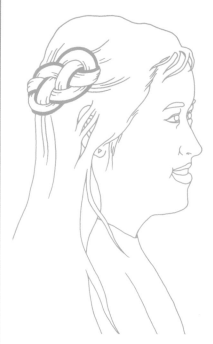

1 Brush the hair to the right, twist into two separate strands and fasten with threads. Make a double coin knot using the double cord technique (see page 11 above). Flip over the body of the knot and fasten with a hair clip, then hide the ends of the hair strands behind the body of the knot. Tie a red cord all the way along the knot body.

3 Use three cords to weave a three-layered hair band. First, bend some steel wire into the shape of a hair band. Tie one cord tightly around the band on a slant. Tie the second cord more loosely onto the band in such a way that the first cord is still visible below it. Fasten the ends of the two cords to the tips of the steel wire with rubber bands. Tie the third cord into a creeper knot (1), starting from the middle of the hair band and working toward the left tip of the wire band. Tie another creeper knot (3) from the middle and work toward the right. Extend the outer loops of the creeper knot lining the left side of the band into a cloverleaf knot (2). Extend the outer loops of the creeper knots lining the right side of the band into a round brocade knot with six outer loops (8), then tie each of the outer loops into a cloverleaf knot (5–7). Extend the outer loops of the creeper knots lining the right side of the band into a cloverleaf knot (11). Make creeper knots up to the right tip of the wire band. Bind both ends of the third cord to the tips of the band with thread. Sew the outer loops of the creeper knots and round brocade knot together, as well as the outer loops of cloverleaf knot 5 and 7, to keep the knot formation firm.

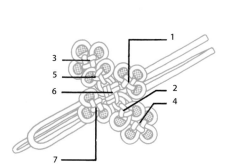

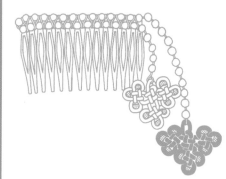

2 String beads on a gold cord, fold it in two uneven lengths and glue it in two rows along the top of a comb, as shown. Hang a *ru yi* knot on each end of the cord. Insert beads in the outer loops.

4 This hairpin is made from silver cord. Fold the cord in half and make a cloverleaf knot (1). Use the right cord to make a cloverleaf knot with two outer loops (2) followed by another cloverleaf knot (4). Use the left cord to make a cloverleaf knot in an anticlockwise direction (7), then another cloverleaf knot with two outer loops (5) followed by a cloverleaf knot (3). Make a ribbon knot (6) and fix cloverleaf knots 1 and 7 onto each loop of the knot, as shown above. Hide one of the remaining cord ends behind the knot body. Tie the remaining cord end into a cloverleaf knot and hide it also behind the knot body. Sew a bead in the middle of the outer loops of each cloverleaf knot. Complete the formation by sliding a hairpin into the back of the ribbon knot.

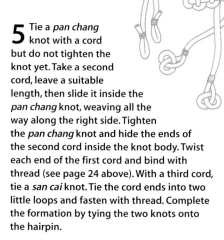

5 Tie a *pan chang* knot with a cord but do not tighten the knot yet. Take a second cord, leave a suitable length, then slide it inside the *pan chang* knot, weaving all the way along the right side. Tighten the *pan chang* knot and hide the ends of the second cord inside the knot body. Twist each end of the first cord and bind with thread (see page 24 above). With a third cord, tie a *san cai* knot. Tie the cord ends into two little loops and fasten with thread. Complete the formation by tying the two knots onto the hairpin.

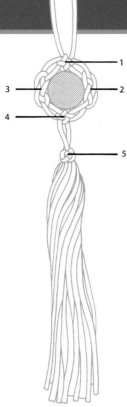

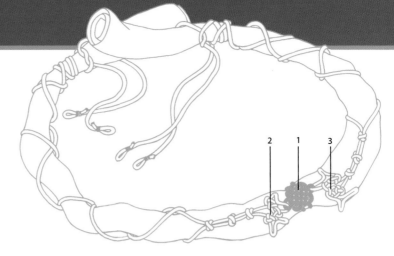

7 To decorate a scarf folded into a roll, tie a cord into a *pan chang* knot (1), then pull both cord ends to the back of the roll and around it and hook them to the outer loops on the top part of the *pan chang* knot. Tie two more cords into separate dragon knots (2, 3) (see *Chinese Knotting*, page 68), hooking up the outer loop on each dragon's head with the corner loops of the *pan chang* knot. Finally, cross wrap the cord ends hanging from the dragon's body around the scarf roll and tie a tight knot at the end of the roll. Fold over each cord end and bind it with thread.

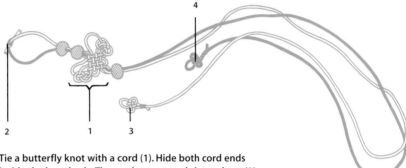

6 Fold a cord and tie a cloverleaf knot (1) at a suitable place, leaving some cord length on both outer loops. String an ornamental bead with both cord ends, then separate them into left and right cords. Tie each cord with the reserved outer loops into a double coin knot (2, 3), then tie the cord ends into a cloverleaf knot (4) at the bottom of the bead. This knot should be tied using the same technique as that of the cloverleaf knot residing in the *ru yi* knot. Finally, make a button tassel (5). Some light colored cords can be added to the tassel cords (see step 2, page 113) for a more colorful tassel.

8 Tie a butterfly knot with a cord (1). Hide both cord ends inside the knot body. Tie another two cords into a knot (2) and string two porcelain beads. Pull both cords through butterfly knot 1 from top to bottom and string a third bead. Tie each cord end into a cloverleaf knot (3, 4) and bind with fine thread. To wear this hair accessory, loop the shorter joined cords above the butterfly knot onto a strand of hair, then pull the cord ends below the third bead to tighten it. Cross wrap both cord ends around the strand of hair and tie them into a knot.

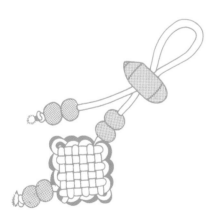

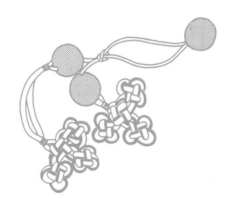

9 Fold a cord and tie a *pan chang* knot, but do not tighten it yet. Pull a cord end from the hair band through the body of the *pan chang* knot, string some beads onto it and then tighten the knot. Take another cord and embellish the rim of the *pan chang* knot, then hide all four cord ends inside the body of the knot.

10 Fold a cotton cord and a plastic cord and tie them into a *ru yi* knot. Hide the ends of the plastic cord in the body of the knot. String three beads onto one of the cotton cord ends, then attach it to the plastic *ru yi* knot. Bind the other end of the cotton cord with thread below its *ru yi* knot but above the first bead.

11 Ordinary fuse wire can be used to make innovative hair clasps. Tie a length of fuse wire into a good luck knot, then gold plate it. Insert love beans into the three outer loops.

HAT ACCESSORIES

See page 30 for photographs of applications 15–21.

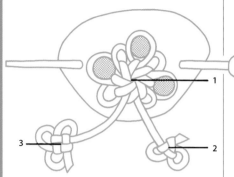

12 Make a piece of artificial leather cord. With the leather side facing out, fold the cord and tie a round brocade knot with six outer loops (1). Then tie one cord end into a cloverleaf knot with two outer loops (2) and the other into a cloverleaf knot with three outer loops (3). Insert three love beans in every second outer loop on the round brocade knot. Glue onto a hair clip.

13 Fold two different colored plastic cords and tie them into a winged *pan chang* knot. Hide all four cord ends inside the knot body. Glue the knot formation onto a hair clip.

14 Tie a plafond knot (see *Chinese Knotting*, page 56) with a thick cord. Hide one cord end inside the knot body. Make a loop with the other one and hide it inside the knot body. Embellish the rim of the plafond knot by weaving and sewing a gold cord into the knot. Insert a bamboo stick or any stick made of wood, metal, plastic or ivory into the two loops.

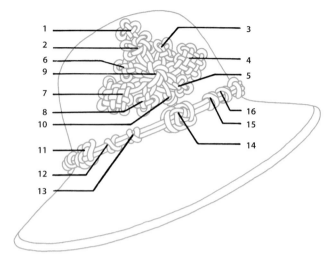

15 This hat decoration comprises a main body decoration and a ring. To make the main body decoration, fold a cord and tie a cloverleaf knot (1) followed by a round brocade knot (2). Then tie another round brocade knot with six outer loops (9). Extend a cloverleaf knot on the first outer loop on the right side (3), a *pan chang* knot on the second outer loop (4) and a cloverleaf knot on the third (5). Repeat this sequence on the outer loops on the left side (6–8), making sure both sides are identical. After completing the round brocade knot, tie a double connection knot (10). Hide the cord ends inside the knot body and sew the formation to the hat.

To make the hat ring, fold a cord, then tie a plafond knot (11) (see *Chinese Knotting*, page 56) followed by two double connection knots (12, 13). Repeat this sequence until the ring is the required length. Hide both cord ends inside the first plafond knot and attach the ring to the hat.

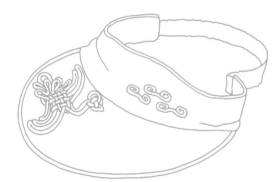

16 The accessory on this sun visor depicts a lucky bird frolicking in the sky, wishing the wearer a safe journey. The tying technique of this lucky bird is basically the same as that of the crane knot (see *Chinese Knotting*, page 80), comprising a *pan chang* body and a two-loop cloverleaf knot neck. However, the double cockscombs and overlapping tail are different. To make the double cockscombs, simply make another round on the cloverleaf knot with two outer loops situated on the head of the crane, as shown here. To make the overlapping tail, take two cord ends and overlap them to form the feathers on the tail. Fold the ends of a few short cords to form "clouds" and sew them onto the sun visor.

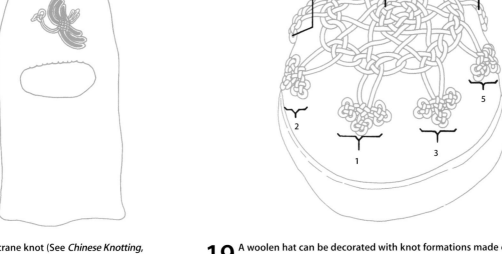

17 Tie a crane knot (See *Chinese Knotting*, page 80). Then take another cord of a similar color and add to the wings, as shown here. This knot can be sewn onto a woolen ski mask.

19 A woolen hat can be decorated with knot formations made of similar colored or contrasting woolen cords. Fold a cord and tie a *ru yi* knot (1). Then begin to tie an eight unity knot (8), a variation of the six unity knot, for the crown. Every time one of the double coin knots on the rim is reached, extend it into a *ru yi* knot (4, 6, 7, 9), thus forming a floral design with eight petals in the form of eight *ru yi* knots. Sew the completed decoration to the woolen hat.

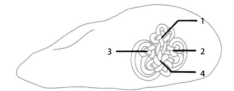

18 French berets made of velvet can be embellished with leather cords for contrast. Fold a cord and tie a cloverleaf knot (1) followed by a round brocade knot with six outer loops (4). When the third outer loop on the right side is tied, bring the cord end back up and tie a double-looped cloverleaf knot (2) with the first outer loop. Repeat on the left (3), making sure both sides are identical. Once the round brocade knot is completed, hide one cord end inside the knot body. To finish the accessory, make a round with the other cord end just below the knot formation, then hide it also inside the knot body. Sew the knot formation to the beret.

20 Tie two plastic cords into two separate butterfly knots. Lengthen the top corner loops on each knot and cut them open, then insert plastic straws, as shown here. Cut the straw ends into fine whiskers. Attach the two butterfly knots to the springy rings on a disco headband.

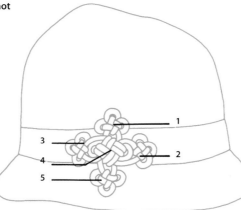

21 This knot formation is made of leather cord, which you may have to cut yourself. With the leather side facing out, fold the cord and tie a cloverleaf knot (1). Make sure the two cord ends are long enough, then separately tie two cloverleaf knots (2, 3). Bring the two cord ends together and tie them into a ribbon knot (4). Adjust the two cloverleaf knots in front of the two outer loops of the ribbon knot. After completing the ribbon knot, hide one cord end inside the knot body. Tie the other into a cloverleaf knot (5), then hide it also inside the knot body.

EARRINGS

See page 31 for photographs of applications 22–25.

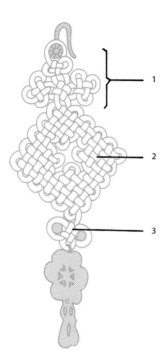

24 This clip-on earring is inset with beads. Fold a cord and tie a round brocade knot. Hide one cord end inside the knot body. Make a loop as big as the outer loops with the other cord end, then hide it inside the knot body. Insert beads in all six loops plus the knot center, then glue the back of the knot to a clip-on earring.

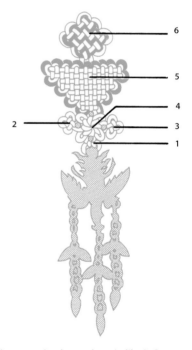

22 Fold a cord and tie a *ru yi* knot (1) followed by a crossed *hui ling* knot (2). Hide one of the cord ends inside the knot body. Hook up the other cord end with the silver ornament and tie a cloverleaf knot (3). Hide the cord end inside the crossed *hui ling* knot. Hook up the earring with the top outer loop of the *ru yi* knot, then sew the silver beads into the two outer loops of the cloverleaf knot, as shown above.

23 By itself, a simple basic knot can be an attractive ornament. A good example is the clip-on earring here. Tie a thick cord into a button knot. Tighten from both sides but not too much. Pull the cord ends to the back and sew them down. Take another gold cord and tie it into an identical knot by following the original weave, then sew it down on top of the original knot. Glue the back of the knot to a clip-on earring.

25 This clip-on earring has a phoenix-like jade ornament at the bottom. Begin the tying process from the tail of the phoenix. Fold a cord and tie a cloverleaf knot (1) followed by a round brocade knot with six outer loops (4). Extend the second outer loop on each side into a cloverleaf knot (2, 3). Then tie a *san cai* knot (5) followed by a *pan chang* knot (6). Do not tighten the latter. Fold a gold cord. Starting from the top part of the *san cai* knot, use the gold cord to embellish the two sides of the knot, then weave it through the whole *pan chang* knot following the left side of the original weave. Tighten the *pan chang* knot and hide the cord ends inside the knot body. Sew the knot formation onto a clip-on earring. Sew the phoenix tail onto the top outer loop of the cloverleaf knot. Finally, sew some beads onto the ornament.

NECKLACES

See page 32 for photographs of applications 26–29.

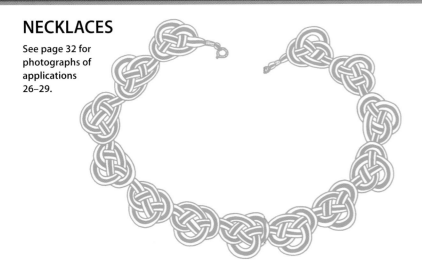

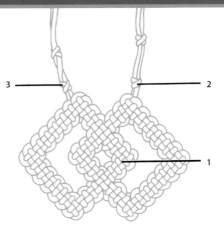

26 This is a three-colored necklace. Normally, when making a knot formation of two or more colors, the first cord would be tied first, then the second cord and so forth following the original weave of the first cord. Since this knot formation is made entirely of double coin knots, which are relatively easy to make and do not get tangled up, two different colored cords can be tied as one, then the third cord woven in. Tie from left to right to a suitable length, then insert a metallic ring and hook at each end of the knot formation.

27 Fold a cord and tie a love knot (1). Pull the cord ends through the right half of the knot and out the top right corner loop. Tie several double connection knots (2) at suitable distances, then tie the cord end into a button receptacle. Pull the other cord through the top left corner loop, fold it and tie the same number of double connection knots (3) at the same distances. Tie a button knot on the end.

28 This necklace comprises an ornamental knot and a necklace loop. To make the ornament, fold a cord and string a bead, leaving a tiny loop at the top of the bead for sewing onto the necklace loop. Then tie a double connection knot (1) followed by a *pan chang* knot (2). After tying the third loop at top right of the *pan chang* knot, extend it into a round brocade knot (3). When the bottom right part is reached, tie a winged *pan chang* knot. Repeat the steps on the left (4), making sure both sides of the knot are identical. Next, fold another cord and embellish the rim of the *pan chang* knot, as shown at left. On reaching the round brocade knots, simply weave through them. Hide the cord ends inside the knot body. Sew some decorative tassels or other item(s) onto the bottom of the knot formation.

To make the necklace loop, fold a thick cord, then tie four plafond knots (5–8) (see *Chinese Knotting*, page 56) from left to right. Leave a suitable space along the cord, then tie another four plafond knots (9–12). Do not tie the knots too tightly yet. Fold another cord and weave the two ends through plafond knots 8–5 and 9–12, then hide the cord ends inside knots 5 and 12. Glue a ring and hook to the two ends of the necklace loop. Finally, sew the ornamental knot onto the necklace loop above the bead.

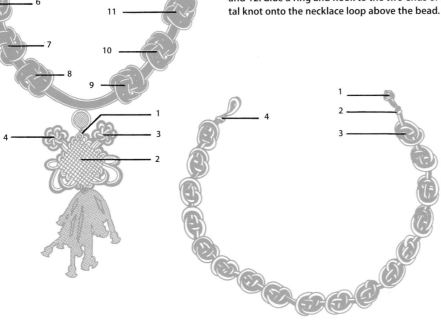

29 Tie a black (or any other color) cord and a gold cord together into a button knot (1) followed by a double connection knot (2). Separate the black and gold cords. Using only the black cord, tie the required number of double coin knots (3) from left to right. To tighten the knots, flip over the necklace, then tighten, but not too tightly. Turn the necklace back over and weave the gold cord through the entire formation. Then, together with the black cord, tie a double connection knot (4). Finally, tie a button loop, turn the cord ends back and sew them into the double connection knot or bind with fine thread.

PENDANTS

See pages 33–37 for photographs of applications 30–50.

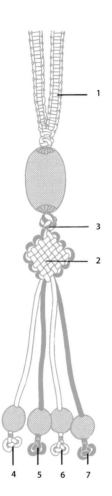

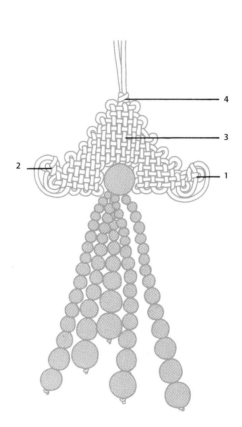

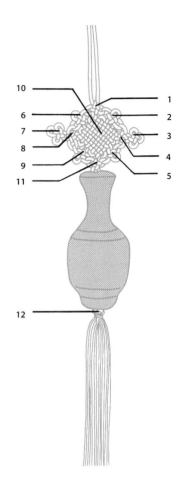

30 This necklace comprises two parts. To make the first part – the necklace loop – tie a series of flat knots (1) (see *Chinese Knotting*, page 58) with three similar colored cords. Make sure the loop is long enough to go over the head, then tie the two ends into another flat knot and bind them tightly together.

To make the second part, fold a cord, leave enough length to string an elongated bead and tie a button knot (2). Do not tighten the knot too much. With the two cord ends, tie a *pan chang* knot (3). Pull another cord through the button knot, then only tighten it. Use the cord ends from the button knot to embellish the rim of the *pan chang* knot. String the four cord ends with a round bead and tie each of the ends into a cloverleaf knot with two outer loops (4–7). Bind each cord end with fine thread. String the length of cord left above the button knot with a big bead and sew it onto the necklace loop.

31 Fold a cord and tie a golden bell knot (3). After completing the first side loop on the bottom right, turn back the cord end and tie a cloverleaf knot with two outer loops, with the last side loop situated on the right slant (1). Repeat on the left side of the knot (2), making sure both sides of the knot formation are identical. On completing the golden bell knot, pull the cord ends through the body and tie a double connection knot (4) on the top of the golden bell knot. Leave enough cord for the necklace loop, then tie a button knot. Bind the cord ends with fine thread. Finally, sew a bead or strings of beads into the empty space at the bottom of the knot formation.

32 Fold a cord, leave a suitable length for the necklace loop, then tie a cloverleaf knot (1). Tie a *pan chang* knot (10) at the bottom of the cloverleaf knot. Extend the middle outer loop on the top right side of the *pan chang* knot into a cloverleaf knot (2), then hook it up with cloverleaf knot (4) tied on the adjoining right corner loop of the *pan chang* knot. Extend the right corner loop of cloverleaf knot 4 into another cloverleaf knot (3). Extend the middle outer loop on the bottom right of the *pan chang* knot into another cloverleaf knot (5) and hook it up with cloverleaf knot 4. Repeat the steps on the left side of the knot formation (6–11), making sure both sides are identical. After completing *pan chang* knot 10, bring the two cord ends together and tie them into a cloverleaf knot (11), then hook them up with the adjoining cloverleaf knots 5 and 9. Finally, pull the two cord ends through the small porcelain vase and tie a button knot (12) to hold it in place.

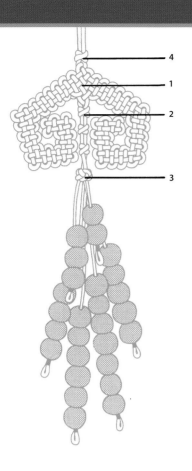

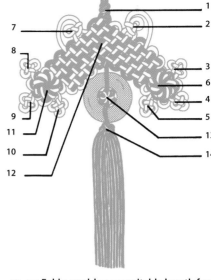

33 The knot formation (1) in this necklace is very unusual. The top comprises a stone chime knot with a series of *hui ling* knots extending from its center. The bottom comprises a left and right cloud formation knot. Using the tying technique of the crossed *hui ling* knot, tie a series of *hui ling* knots, then, using the tying technique of the cloud formation knot, tie the stone chime knot and the left and right cloud formation knots. After completing knot formation 1, tie three double connection knots (2) and a button knot (3). Fold two cords and sew them onto the bottom of the button knot to give another four cord ends. String all six cord ends with beads. Hook another cord through the top corner loop of the stone chime knot and tie a double connection knot (4). Leave enough cord for the necklace loop, then tie a button knot.

35 Fold a cord, leave a suitable length for the necklace loop, then tie a double connection knot (1) followed by a stone chime knot (12). Extend a round brocade knot with six outer loops on each outer loop on the bottom left and right of the stone chime knot (6, 11). Do not tighten the knot too much. Weave a gold cord along the right of the stone chime knot. After completing the third outer loop, turn back the cord and tie a cloverleaf knot (2) together with the second side loop. On reaching round brocade knot 6, tie a cloverleaf knot on every second outer loop (3–5). Repeat the steps on the left (7–10), making sure both sides are identical. After the gold cord has been woven through the stone chime knot, tighten the knot body and hide the gold cord inside. Pull the original cord ends down both sides of the jade ring into the center and tie a round brocade knot (13). Finally, tie a button knot (14).

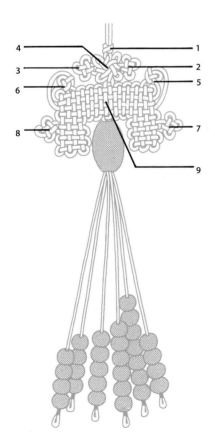

34 Fold a cord, leave a suitable length for the necklace loop, then tie a double connection knot (1) followed by a round brocade knot with six outer loops (4). Extend the middle outer loop on each side of the round brocade knot into a cloverleaf knot (2, 3). Use both cord ends to tie a *bao men* knot (9). After completing the first side loop on the right side, turn back the cord end and tie a two-loop cloverleaf knot (5) together with the side loop nearest the top right corner loop. Do exactly the same on the top left side (6). After completing the second last side loop on the right side, extend it into a cloverleaf knot (7). Repeat on the left side (8), making sure both sides are identical. After completing *bao men* knot 9, string the cord ends emerging from the bottom of the knot with a big bead. Fold another two cords and sew them onto the two cord ends at the base of the bead to make six cord ends. Finally, string each of the six cord ends with beads.

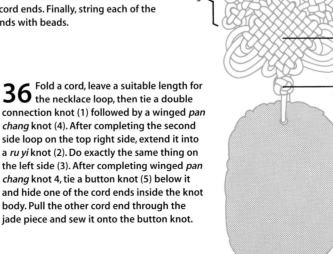

36 Fold a cord, leave a suitable length for the necklace loop, then tie a double connection knot (1) followed by a winged *pan chang* knot (4). After completing the second side loop on the top right side, extend it into a *ru yi* knot (2). Do exactly the same thing on the left side (3). After completing winged *pan chang* knot 4, tie a button knot (5) below it and hide one of the cord ends inside the knot body. Pull the other cord end through the jade piece and sew it onto the button knot.

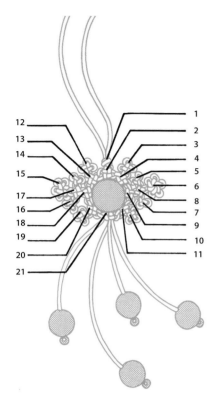

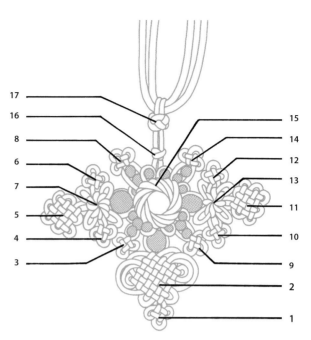

38 Start this knot formation from the base. Fold a cord and tie a cloverleaf knot (1) followed by a winged *pan chang* knot (2). Start tying a round brocade knot with fourteen outer loops (15). Extend the second outer loop on the left into a cloverleaf knot (3). Extend the fourth outer loop into a round brocade knot with six outer loops (7), and extend the first, third and fifth outer loops of the round brocade knot into a cloverleaf knot (4), a *pan chang* knot (5) and a cloverleaf knot (6) respectively, as shown above. Extend the sixth outer loop into a cloverleaf knot (8). Repeat the steps on the right side of the knot formation (9–15), making sure both sides are identical. After completing round brocade knot 15, bring the cord ends together and tie a double connection knot (16) followed by a button knot (17). Finally, sew beads of different sizes inside the loops of the round brocade knot, as shown above.

37 Fold a cord, leave a suitable length for the necklace loop, then tie a double connection knot (1) followed by a cloverleaf knot (2). Separate out the right cord end and tie a cloverleaf knot (3). Place it on the middle outer loop of another cloverleaf knot (4), then hook up the outer loops of cloverleaf knots 4 and 2. Then tie a knot similar to a *ru yi* knot (8) by replacing its topmost cloverleaf knot with a round brocade knot (6). The left and right sides of the *ru yi* knot are both cloverleaf knots with two outer loops (5, 7). On the bottom of the *ru yi* knot, tie a cloverleaf knot (9) that is hooked up with cloverleaf knot 4, as shown. Then tie another two cloverleaf knots (10, 11) using the same tying technique as that of cloverleaf knots 3 and 4. Repeat the steps on the left side of the knot formation (12–20), making sure both sides are identical. Bring the two cord ends together and tie a cloverleaf knot (21). Sew a pair of folded cords onto the base of the knot formation. String each of the four cords with a bead and sew a tiny bead onto the ends. Finally, insert a big bead in the center of the knot formation.

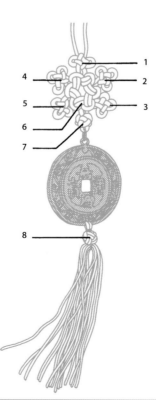

39 Fold a cord, leave a suitable length for the necklace loop, then tie a cloverleaf knot (1) followed by a good luck knot with four outer loops (6). Extend each outer loop into a cloverleaf knot (2–5). Bring the cord ends together and tie a button knot (7). Pull the cord ends through the loop at the top of an old coin, then turn them back and sew them onto the button knot. Make a button tassel (8) and attach it to the bottom loop of the coin.

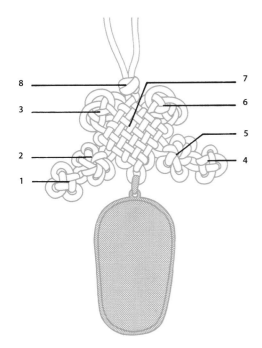

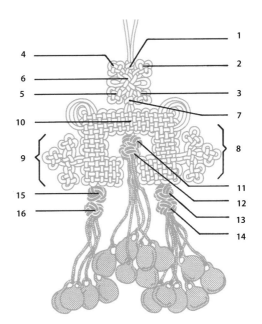

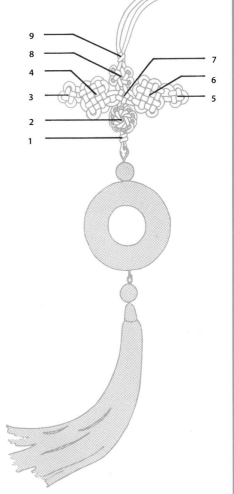

40 Start this knot formation from the base. Pull a cord through the loop at the top of a porcelain medallion (or other ornament), fold it and tie a *pan chang* knot (7). After completing the second side loop on the top right side, extend it into a round brocade knot (2) and then extend the outermost outer loop into a cloverleaf knot (1). After completing the second side loop on the bottom right side, tie a double coin knot (3) together with the first side loop. Repeat the steps on the left of the knot formation (4–6), making sure both sides are identical. After completing *pan chang* knot 7, bring the cord ends together and tie a double connection knot (8). Leave enough cord for the necklace loop, then tie the ends into a button knot.

41 Fold a cord, leave a suitable length for the necklace loop, then tie a double connection knot (1) followed by a round brocade knot with six outer loops (6). Extend every second outer loop of the round brocade knot into a cloverleaf knot (2–5). After completing the round brocade knot, tie a double connection knot (7) before starting a special variation of the *bao men* knot (10). Using the tying technique of the cloud formation knot, tie the bottom left and right parts that bend inward. Using the tying technique of the winged *pan chang* knot, tie the top left and right corner loops, as well as their nearby side loops. Extend the second last side loop on each side into a *ru yi* knot (8, 9). After completing special *bao men* knot 10, tie the cord ends into two button knots (11, 12) and insert them inside the center space of the knot. Pull the cords through the two wings at the bottom of the formation and make two more button knots (13–15) with each. Finally, add strings of beads and small bells to the bottom of the button knots, as shown above.

42 Start this knot formation from the base. Pull a cord through a hook attached to a medallion (or other ornament), fold it and tie a double connection knot (1) followed by a round brocade knot with eight outer loops (2). Separate the cord ends. Tie the right one into a *pan chang* knot (4) and extend the loop on the right side into a cloverleaf knot (3). Repeat the steps with the left cord end (6, 5). Bring the cord ends together and tie a cloverleaf knot (7) using the tying technique of a *ru yi* knot with a cloverleaf knot within it. Then tie another round brocade knot (8) followed by a double connection knot (9). Leave a suitable length for the necklace loop, then tie the ends into a button knot. Finally, sew beads in the center and in the outer loops of both round brocade knots.

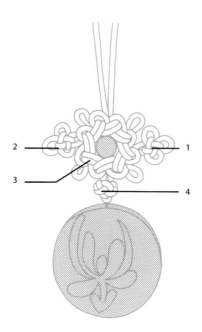

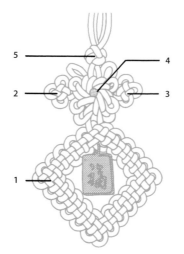

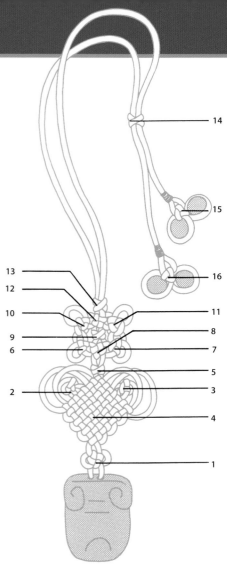

43 Fold a cord and tie each end into a cloverleaf knot (not shown). Leave enough length for the necklace loop. Bring the cord ends together and tie a good luck knot with six outer loops (3). Extend the middle outer loops on each side of the good luck knot into a cloverleaf knot (1, 2). Bring the cord ends together at the bottom of the good luck knot and tie them into a button knot (4). Pull the cord ends through the loop of a porcelain medallion (or other suitable ornament), fold them back and and sew them onto the body of the button knot. Finally, sew a bead in the center of the good luck knot.

44 Fold a cord and tie a *hui ling* knot (1) followed by a round brocade knot with ten outer loops (4). Extend the middle outer loop on each side into a cloverleaf knot (2, 3). After completing the round brocade knot, bring the cord ends together and tie a button knot (5). Fold another cord and sew it onto the button knot to make a double-layer necklace loop. Decorate the loop with gold threads at suitable distances. Finally, sew a gold medallion onto the *hui ling* knot.

46 This necklace comprises an axe-like knot and a ram's head knot which, when combined, denote good luck. Fold a cord through a piece of jade and tie a cloverleaf knot (1) followed by a winged *pan chang* knot (4). Extend the outer loops on each side of the winged structure into a cloverleaf knot (2, 3) followed by a double connection knot (5). Separate the two cord ends and tie each into a cloverleaf knot with two outer loops (6, 7). In between knots 6 and 7, tie another cloverleaf knot (8) using the tying technique of the last cloverleaf knot within the *ru yi* knot. Tie knots (9–12) in exactly the same way as knots 5–8. Remember to hook up the adjoining outer loops of the top and bottom cloverleaf knots. Tie a double connection knot (13) at the top. Leave enough cord for the necklace loop, then tie another double connection knot (14). Tie each cord end into a cloverleaf knot (15, 16) and bind with thread. Finally, insert beads in the outer loops of cloverleaf knots 15 and 16.

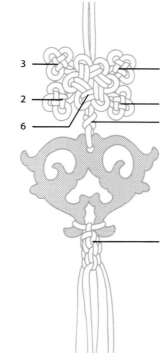

45 Pull a cord through the top of the pendant, fold it and tie a double connection knot (1). Separate the cord ends and tie the right cord end into two consecutive cloverleaf knots (2, 3), leaving a suitable distance between them. Do the same with the left cord end (4, 5). Bring the cord ends together and tie a good luck knot with four outer loops (6). Extend each outer loop of the good luck knot into the adjacent cloverleaf knots. Leave enough cord for the necklace loop, then tie a button knot. Finally, make a good luck tassel (7) and tie it to the bottom of the pendant.

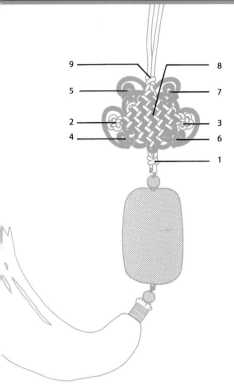

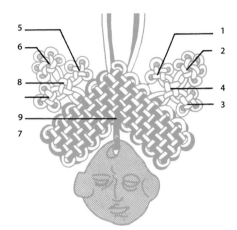

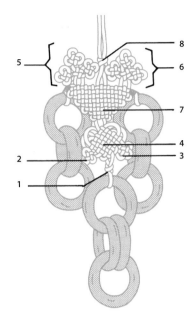

47 Fold a cord through the loop of a pendant and tie a double connection knot (1) followed by a *pan chang* knot (8). Extend the outer corner loop on each side of the *pan chang* knot into a cloverleaf knot (2, 3), but do not tighten the *pan chang* knot yet. Tie a gold cord along the right side of the original cord in the *pan chang* knot. On completing the top right corner loop, turn the gold cord end back and tie a cloverleaf knot with two outer loops (4), the first side loop being on the top right side. On completing the bottom right corner loop of the *pan chang* knot, turn the cord end back and tie a cloverleaf knot with two outer loops (5), the first side loop being on the bottom right side. Repeat the steps on the left (6, 8), making sure both sides of the knot formation are identical. Then tighten the *pan chang* knot. Hide the gold cord end inside the bottom part of the knot body. Then tie the two original cord ends into a double connection knot (9). Leave enough cord for the necklace loop and tie the ends into a button knot. Finally, sew jade (or other) beads into the two outer loops of cloverleaf knots 2 and 3.

48 Gold cords are not normally used to tie the body of a knot since they snap quite easily. This knot formation is an exception. Using soft cords to supplement a gold cord prevents it from being damaged by excessive friction. First, fold a gold cord and tie a stone chime knot (9). Extend the third loops on the top left and top right sides into knots similar to a *ru yi* knot by replacing the cloverleaf knot situated on top of the *ru yi* knot with a round brocade knot (2–4; 6–8). Do not tighten the stone chime knot yet. Weave another soft cord into the knot body for support, then only tighten the knot. After completing the stone chime knot, hook up the green gemstone pendant with the soft cord. Pull the soft cord and the gold cord together upward through the knot body. Tie the right ends of both cords into several interspaced double connection knots to form the necklace loop. Do the same for the left cord ends. Then tie the two ends of the necklace loop into a button knot. Finally, insert beads into the outer loops of the *ru yi* knots, as shown.

49 Fold a cord through a chain of jade rings and tie a double connection knot (1) followed by a winged *pan chang* knot (4). Extend the second side loops on the top left and right of the winged *pan chang* knot into a cloverleaf knot (2, 3). Then tie a *san cai* knot (7), making the bottom corner loops on each side fold around the chain of jade rings. Extend the first side loops on the bottom left and right into a *ru yi* knot (5, 6). Tie another double connection knot (8). Leave enough cord for the necklace loop, then tie the two ends into a final double connection knot.

50 First, make a piece of leather cord. With the leather side facing out, pass the cord through a passage at the top of the porcelain medallion, then tie a round brocade knot with six outer loops (3). Extend the middle outer loop on each side of the round brocade knot into a cloverleaf knot (1, 2). Leave enough cord for the necklace loop, then tie both cord ends together. Finally, insert a bead in the center of the round brocade knot.

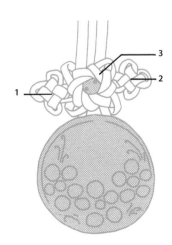

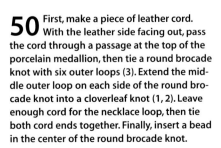

CLOTHING ACCENTS

See pages 38–44 for photographs of applications 51–79.

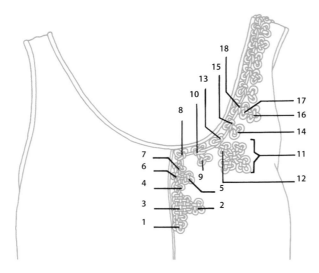

51 Start the knot formation on this evening gown at the bottom. Fold a cord into two unequal lengths and tie a cloverleaf knot (1) followed by the right-hand side of a prosperity knot (3). Extend the top right side loop of the prosperity knot into a cloverleaf knot (2). After completing the prosperity knot, tie another cloverleaf knot (4). Separate the cord ends and tie the right one into a cloverleaf knot (5). Bring both cord ends together and tie another cloverleaf knot (6), then another (7). Then tie a series of equally spaced creeper knots. Hook up cloverleaf knot 7 with the outer loop of creeper knot (8). Extend the outer loop of creeper knot (10) into a cloverleaf knot with two outer loops (9). Extend the outer loop of creeper knot (13) into a cloverleaf knot (12), then extend the top outer loop into a *ru yi* knot (11). Extend the outer loop of creeper knot (15) into a cloverleaf knot with two outer loops (14). Extend the outer loop of creeper knot (18) into a cloverleaf knot (17), and extend the outer loop into another cloverleaf knot (16). For the rest of the creeper knots, tie their outer loops into alternating two outer-loop cloverleaf knots and plain cloverleaf knots. After completing the knot formation, sew it down the front and around the neckline of an evening gown (or day dress).

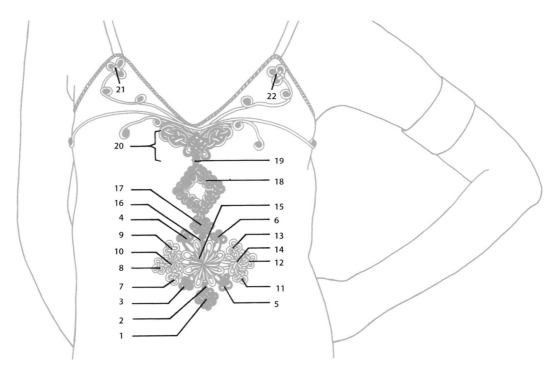

52 Start the knot formation on this evening gown from the bottom. Fold a cord and tie a *pan chang* knot (1) followed by a double connection knot (2). Then tie a round brocade knot with fourteen outer loops (15). Extend the second and sixth outer loops on the right side into cloverleaf knots (3, 4). Repeat on the left side (5, 6), making sure that both sides are identical. Weave a gold cord into round brocade knot 15 and tie an outer loop in between every second cloverleaf knot, as shown above. Extend the fourth outer loop on each side into a round brocade knot with six outer loops (10, 14). Extend a cloverleaf knot in between every second outer loop (7–9; 11–13). After completing the weaving, hide the gold cord ends inside the knot body. Use the original cord ends to tie a double connection knot (16), a *pan chang* knot (17), a *hui ling* knot (18), a double connection knot (19) and a butterfly knot (20). Weave two more gold cords into the inner side of the *hui ling* knot and the butterfly knot, as shown above. After completing two rounds with the gold cord ends, tie each into a cloverleaf knot (21, 22). With another two gold cords, decorate the gown with curved lines and circles, as shown. Finally, sew pieces of the original cord inside the circles on the curved lines.

53 Use two different colored cords – one dark and one light – to trim the edges of the sailor collar on this blouse, starting at the front left opening (see page 39). Sew in place parallel rows of cords, the lighter one along the outer edge, the darker one on the inner side. At the back of the sailor collar, tie a *ru yi* knot (1, 2) on each corner using the darker of the two cords. Make sure you start with enough cord for the trimming and the knots.

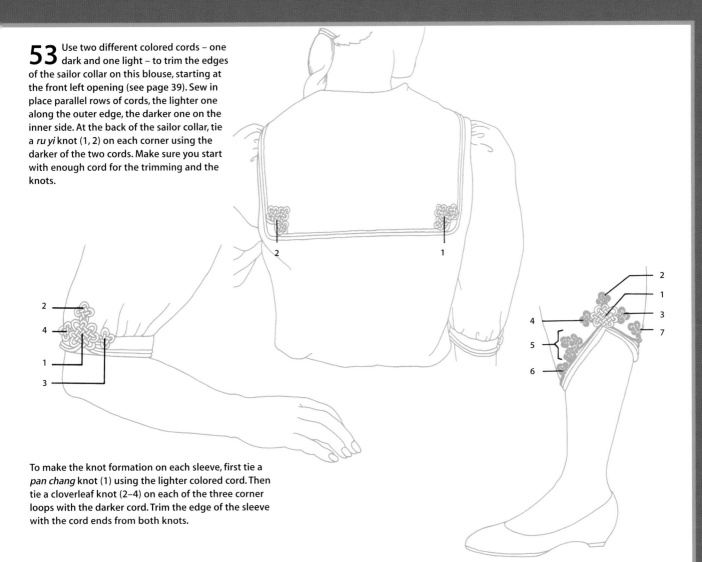

To make the knot formation on each sleeve, first tie a *pan chang* knot (1) using the lighter colored cord. Then tie a cloverleaf knot (2–4) on each of the three corner loops with the darker cord. Trim the edge of the sleeve with the cord ends from both knots.

To decorate the trouser slits, first tie the lighter colored cord into a *pan chang* knot (1). Then, with the darker cord, tie a cloverleaf knot (2–4) on each of the three corner loops of the *pan chang* knot. Trim the edges of the trouser legs with the ends of the lighter colored cord. Use the ends of the darker cord to tie a *ru yi* knot (5, 7) on each side of the main knot formation followed by a cloverleaf knot (6; 8 not shown) before continuing to lay down the cord ends inside the lighter trim.

54 Make two leather cords. With the leather side facing out, tie the first cord into two cloverleaf knots (1, 2) followed by a *ru yi* knot (3) and three cloverleaf knots (4–6). Repeat the steps (7–12) on the other side with the second cord. Sew the knot formations onto the lapels of the jacket, as shown at left, then pull the cord ends to the back of the lapels and tie them into cloverleaf knots.

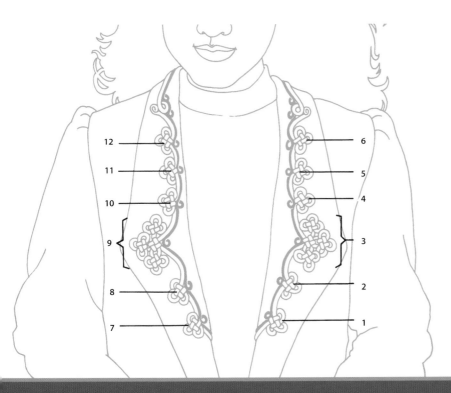

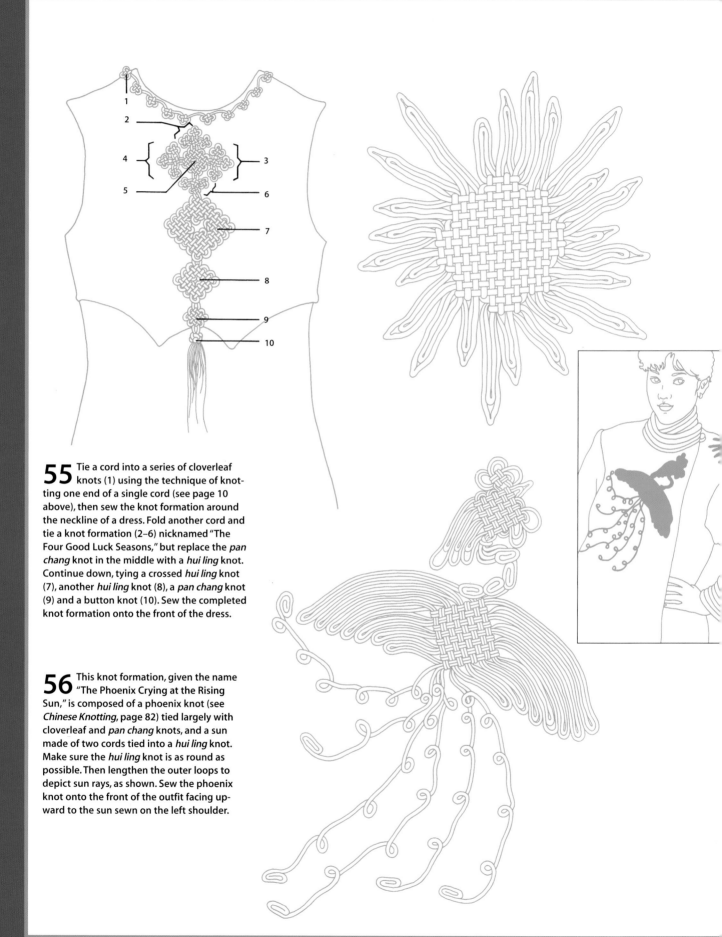

55 Tie a cord into a series of cloverleaf knots (1) using the technique of knotting one end of a single cord (see page 10 above), then sew the knot formation around the neckline of a dress. Fold another cord and tie a knot formation (2–6) nicknamed "The Four Good Luck Seasons," but replace the *pan chang* knot in the middle with a *hui ling* knot. Continue down, tying a crossed *hui ling* knot (7), another *hui ling* knot (8), a *pan chang* knot (9) and a button knot (10). Sew the completed knot formation onto the front of the dress.

56 This knot formation, given the name "The Phoenix Crying at the Rising Sun," is composed of a phoenix knot (see *Chinese Knotting*, page 82) tied largely with cloverleaf and *pan chang* knots, and a sun made of two cords tied into a *hui ling* knot. Make sure the *hui ling* knot is as round as possible. Then lengthen the outer loops to depict sun rays, as shown. Sew the phoenix knot onto the front of the outfit facing upward to the sun sewn on the left shoulder.

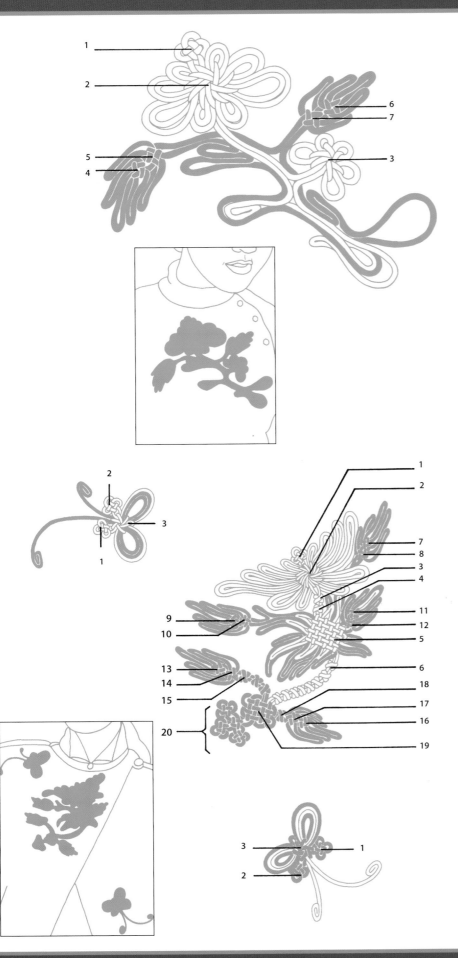

57 This flower-shaped knot, made from red and green leather cords, makes an attractive accessory on a black woolen sweater. To form the flower, fold the red leather cord and tie a cloverleaf knot (1) followed by a round brocade knot with eight outer loops (2). Tie another round in every outer loop of the round brocade knot. Cut off and hide the end of the left cord inside the body of the flower. Tie the right cord into another round brocade knot (3) a short distance below the flower, to form the bud. Twist the remaining right cord into a stalk shape and then hide the end under the flower. Sew the bud and stalk onto the sweater. Next, tie the green leather cord into two cloverleaf knots (4, 5; 6, 7), lengthening the outer loops to form a leaf shape. Twist both remaining green cord ends into the shape of a leaf stalk along the outer edges of the red stalk and sew onto the garment.

58 To make this exceptional floral design, first fold a red cord and tie a cloverleaf knot (1) followed by a round brocade knot with ten outer loops (2). Tie another round within each outer loop of the round brocade knot, lengthening the loops, as shown at left. Continue downward, tying two double connection knots (3, 4) and a *pan chang* knot (5) also with its outer loops lengthened, as shown. Then tie eight double connection knots (6) to form the flower stalk.

For the leaves, start at top right. Tie a green cord into two cloverleaf knots (7, 8), lengthening and extending their outer loops to form branches. Continue downward, using the right cord to form another leaf (9, 10) and to lay down loops around *pan chang* knot 5, and the left cord to form another leaf (11, 12) with lengthened branches and for embellishment. Use another green cord to form the second leaf (13, 14) on the left, then tie three double connection knots (15) below it. Tie a double connection knot (18) below the third leaf (16, 17) on the lower right to make the flower stalk look thicker. Tie a *pan chang* knot (19) below the flower stalk. Hide one of the remanning cord ends inside the knot body, then tie the other one into a *ru yi* knot (20). Hide that cord end also inside the knot body.

To make the butterfly, tie a red cord into a round brocade knot (3). Extend the second outer loop on each side into a cloverleaf knot (1, 2). Then decorate the butterfly with a green cord, as shown. Tie another butterfly using exactly the same technique, but this time reverse the color scheme. After completing the flower and the two butterflies, sew them onto the jacket (or other garment).

59 The entire rim on the cheongsam at left is trimmed with cords and knots. Tie a *ru yi* knot on the bottom of each outer sleeve and the slits at the sides of the cheongsam. Sew a *ru yi* knot and a *pan chang* knot onto the front of the cheongsam to act as a knot button and loop.

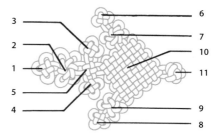

60 Fold a cord and tie a cloverleaf knot (1) followed by a round brocade knot (2). Separate the cord ends and tie each into a cloverleaf knot (3, 4). Then tie both cord ends into a cloverleaf knot (5) in the center of knots 3 and 4 using the tying technique of the cloverleaf knot within the *ru yi* knot, followed by a *pan chang* knot (10). After completing the third side loop on the top right part of the *pan chang* knot, extend it into a round brocade knot (7), and then extend the outermost loop into a cloverleaf knot (6). Repeat the steps on the left of the *pan chang* knot (8, 9), making sure both sides are identical. After completing *pan chang* knot 10, tie a button knot (11) and hide both cord ends inside the knot body.

61 Fold a cord, leave a suitable length for the button loop, then tie a winged *pan chang* knot. Hide both cord ends inside the knot body.

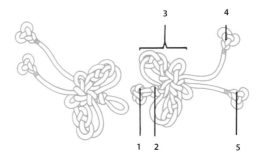

62 This pair comprises a knot button and loop. To make the knot button (above right), fold a cord and tie a button knot (1) to form the button, followed by a double connection knot (2). Then tie a butterfly knot (3), but replace the *pan chang* knot in the middle with a round brocade knot. Tie each cord end into a cloverleaf knot with two loops (4, 5). Fold back the cord ends and bind them below the knots with gold thread. To make the button loop (above left), fold another cord, leave a suitable length for the button loop, then tie a double connection knot and a butterfly knot. Tie each cord end into a cloverleaf knot with two loops, then fold back the cord ends and bind them below the knots with gold thread.

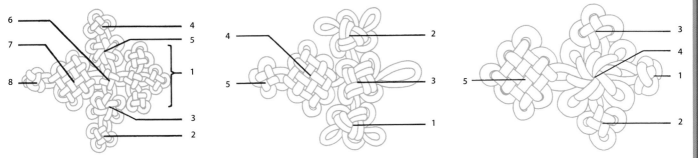

63 First tie a *ru yi* knot (1). Separate the cord ends and tie the right one into a round brocade knot (3). Extend its outermost loop into a cloverleaf knot (2). Repeat the steps using the left cord end (4, 5). Then tie a cloverleaf knot (6) using the tying technique of the cloverleaf knot within the *ru yi* knot. Continue downward, tying a *pan chang* knot (7) and a button knot (8). Hide both cord ends inside the knot body.

64 Fold a cord, leaving a suitable length for the button loop. Tie each cord end into a good luck knot with two outer loops (1, 2). Then tie both cord ends into a good luck knot (3) in the middle. Hook up good luck knots 1 and 2 with the left and right outer loops of 3. Continue downward, tying a *pan chang* knot (4). Hide one cord end inside the knot body. Tie the other cord end into a cloverleaf knot (5) and also hide its end inside the knot body.

65 Fold a cord and tie a button knot (1) to form a button, followed by a round brocade knot with six outer loops (4). Extend the middle outer loop on each side into a cloverleaf knot (2, 3). After completing the round brocade knot, tie a *pan chang* knot (5). Hide both cord ends inside the knot body.

66 Fold a cord and tie a button knot (1) to form the button, followed by a round brocade knot with fourteen outer loops (8). After completing the second outer loop, extend it into a cloverleaf knot (2). Extend the fourth outer loop into a *pan chang* knot (3) and the sixth outer loop into a cloverleaf knot (4). Repeat the steps on the other side (5–7), making sure both sides are identical. After completing the round brocade knot, tie a *pan chang* knot (9). Hide both cord ends inside the knot body.

67 Fold a cord, leaving a suitable length for the button loop, then tie a winged *pan chang* knot. Hide the cord ends inside the body of the knot.

68 This decorative knot is a variation of the fish knot (see *Chinese Knotting*, page 84), but the first double connection knot on the tail is omitted. Only the modified *pan chang* knot of the fish is tied. Lengthen the two outer loops on the left side to form the tail. After completing the knot body, pull the cord ends through the body and tie another round in the tail, as shown, then hide the ends inside the body.

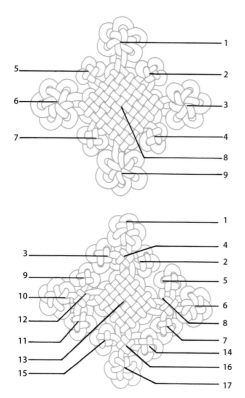

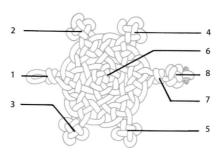

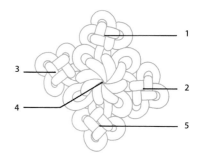

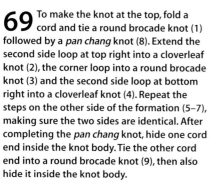

70 Ancient Chinese called the tortoise "Suen Wu," hence this tortoise-like knot is called the Suen Wu knot. Fold a cord, leave a loop, then tie a double connection knot (1) to form the tail, followed by a six unity knot (6). Extend the two double connection knots on each side into two more double connection knots to form the four legs (2, 4; 3, 5). The six unity knot becomes the body of the tortoise. The head is formed by a double connection knot (7) and a button knot (8). Hide one cord end inside the knot body. Turn back the other cord to make the mouth, as shown above, then sew it onto the button knot. Finally, sew beads onto the tortoise's head to make the eyes.

71 Fold a cord and tie a cloverleaf knot (1) followed by a round brocade knot with six loops (4). Extend the middle outer loop on each side into a cloverleaf knot (2, 3). After completing the round brocade knot, hide one cord end inside the knot body and tie the other one into a cloverleaf knot (5), then hide the end of that also.

69 To make the knot at the top, fold a cord and tie a round brocade knot (1) followed by a *pan chang* knot (8). Extend the second side loop at top right into a cloverleaf knot (2), the corner loop into a round brocade knot (3) and the second side loop at bottom right into a cloverleaf knot (4). Repeat the steps on the other side of the formation (5–7), making sure the two sides are identical. After completing the *pan chang* knot, hide one cord end inside the knot body. Tie the other cord end into a round brocade knot (9), then also hide it inside the knot body.

The knot formation at the bottom is similar to the "Four Good Luck Seasons" (see project 55, page 134), except that the cloverleaf knot on top of each *ru yi* knot is replaced by a round brocade knot.

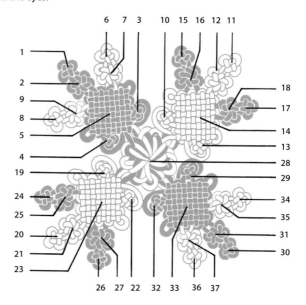

72 This complex decorative knot comprises four similar knot formations surrounding a central round brocade knot with ten outer loops. First, fold a dark colored cord and tie a cloverleaf knot (1), a round brocade knot (2) and a *pan chang* knot (5). On completing the last side loop at bottom right, turn back the cord and tie a cloverleaf knot (3) with the middle side loop. Do the same on the left side (4). Once the *pan chang* knot is completed, pull a light colored knot through the top right side and out the top left side of the knot. Tie the right cord end into a round brocade knot (7) and extend its top outer loop into a cloverleaf knot (6). Then pull this cord end through the knot body to unite it with the dark colored cord end at the bottom of *pan chang* knot 5. Repeat the steps with the left end of the light colored cord (8, 9). On completing the formation, tie the light colored cord ends into a round brocade knot (28) with ten outer loops. Extend the middle outer loops on the right, left and bottom of round brocade knot 28 into a formation similar to steps 1–5 above. Do not tighten round brocade knot 28 too

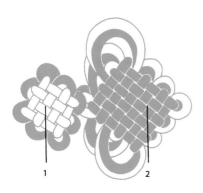

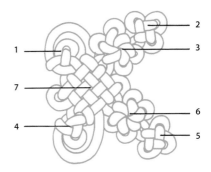

74 Fold a cord and tie a *pan chang* knot (7). On completing the first loop at top right, turn back the cord ends and tie a round brocade knot (3), hooking it up with the neighboring side loop (1). Then extend the outermost loop into a cloverleaf knot (2). On completing the first side loop at bottom right, extend it into a round brocade knot (6), hooking it up with the neighboring side loop (4). Then extend the outermost loop into a cloverleaf knot (5). Make sure the right and left sides are identical. After completing the *pan chang* knot, sew the cord ends inside the knot body.

73 This decorative knot formation is made with two cords. Tie the first cord into a *pan chang* knot (1), then embellish its rim with the second cord. After completing the rim embellishment, tie the second cord into a winged *pan chang* knot (2) and use the first cord to embellish its rim. Hide all four cord ends inside the body of the knot.

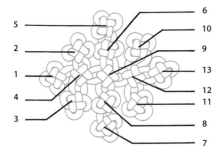

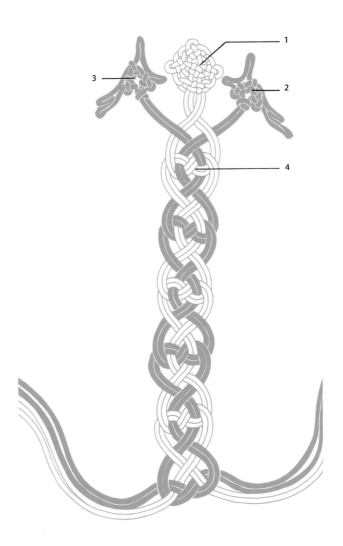

75 This knot formation comprises a series of interlinked cloverleaf knots tied in the sequence (1–13), as indicated above. However, the tying techniques of cloverleaf knots 4, 9 and 12 are the same as that of the last cloverleaf knot within the *ru yi* knot.

tightly yet. Weave the right end of the dark colored cord beneath *pan chang* knot 5 into round brocade knot 28, as shown. On completing the middle outer loop on the right, pull the cord end through the body of *pan chang* knot 14 and tie knots 15–18 using the same technique as for knots 6–9. Do exactly the same thing with the dark colored cord's left cord end. After the dark colored cord ends are finished, tighten and adjust round brocade knot 28. Continue downward, tying a structure similar to knots 1– 9.

76 The design of this formation, "Two Dragons Playing With a Dragon Ball," is based on a stone carving on the wall of an ancient Chinese tomb. It is tied with cords of two different colors. First, fold a cord and tie a round brocade knot (1) to form the dragon ball. Then, using the tying technique of the dragon knot (see *Chinese Knotting*, page 68), tie the two cords separately into two dragon heads (2, 3) lying on either side of the round brocade knot. Finally, using the tying technique with four cord ends (see page 13 above), tie a long series of knots (4) very similar to a double connection knot to form the intertwined bodies of the dragons.

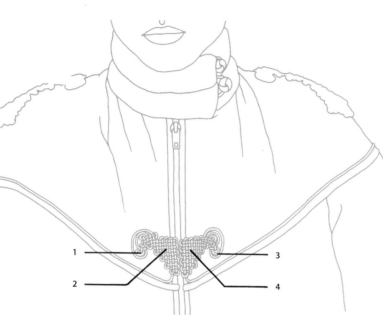

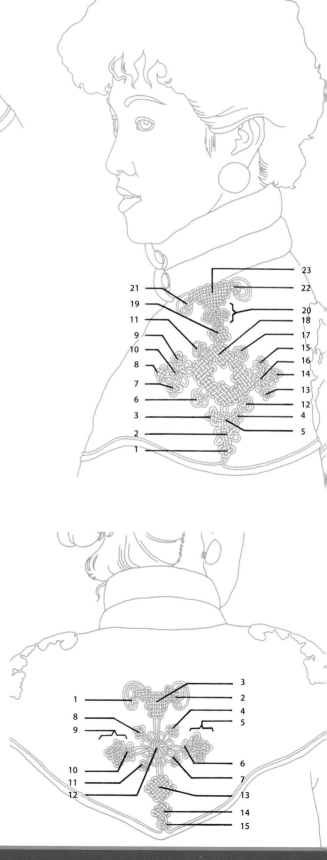

77 To make the knot formation on the front of the jacket (see diagram above), fold a cord and tie the right half of a *san cai* knot (2). Tie the adjoining side loops at the right corner into a cloverleaf knot with two outer loops (1). Using another cord, repeat the steps for the left side (3, 4), making sure the knots are identical. The two halves when placed on either side of the zipper opening form a ram's head.

To make two identical knot formations for the shoulders (see diagram at right), start knotting from the bottom. Fold a cord and tie a cloverleaf knot (1) followed by a round brocade knot (2). Separate the cord ends and tie each into a cloverleaf knot (3, 4). Bring the cord ends together and tie another cloverleaf knot (5) using the tying technique of the cloverleaf knot situated in the middle of a *ru yi* knot. Then tie a crossed *hui ling* knot (18). Extend the side loops on all four sides of the *hui ling* knot into a double coin knot (6, 11; 12, 17). Extend the right corner loop into a round brocade knot with six outer loops (10). Extend every second outer loop of the round brocade knot into a cloverleaf knot (7–9). Repeat the last two steps on the other side (13–16), making sure the left and right sides of the formation are identical. After completing crossed *hui ling* knot 18, tie a *pan chang* knot (19), a *ru yi* knot (20) and, finally, a knot similar to the ram's head structure (21–23) on the back of the jacket (see above).

To make the knot formation on the back (see diagram at right), first fold a cord and tie a *san cai* knot (3). Tie the adjoining side loops at the top left corner into a cloverleaf knot with two outer loops (1). Repeat on the other side (2), making sure both sides are identical. After completing the *san cai* knot, pull the cord ends through the *san cai* knot body and tie a round brocade knot with fourteen outer loops (12). Extend the second outer loop on the right side into a cloverleaf knot (4). Extend the fourth outer loop into a round brocade knot (6), then extend its outermost loop into a *ru yi* knot (5). Extend the sixth outer loop of round brocade knot 12 into a cloverleaf knot (7). Repeat the steps on the left (8–11), making sure both sides are identical. After completing round brocade knot 12, tie a big *pan chang* knot (13), a small *pan chang* knot (14) and a cloverleaf knot (15).

Sew all four knot formations onto the jacket. Using the cord ends from the formations on the front and back of the jacket, trim the edges, moving towards both shoulders, as shown, then hide all the cord ends below the knot bodies on the shoulders.

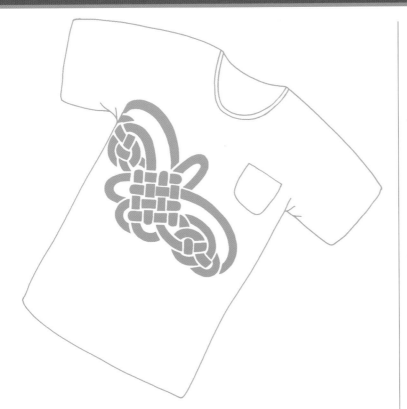

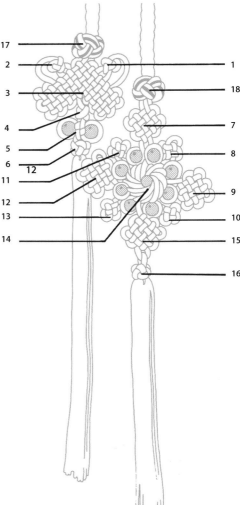

See pages 45–47 for photographs
of applications 80–88.

78 A variation on using knotted cords is to simply print Chinese knots on clothes. First, draw a butterfly (or any other) knot on a piece of cardboard. Then, using a sharp cutting knife, cut out the parts to receive the color. Lay the cardboard template on a suitable place on the garment. Spray, brush or dab paint or dye on the empty spaces in the template. Alternatively, paint the knot pattern directly on the garment without using a cardboard template.

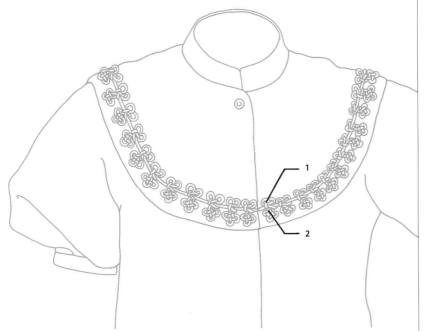

79 Use the tying technique employing one cord end (see page 10 above), tie a long series of creeper knots on both sides of the cord. Extend the outer loop of each creeper knot (1) into a cloverleaf knot (2). On completing the desired length, sew the knot formation onto the front of the dress, as shown above.

80 This ornament comprises two knot formations hanging from a belt. To make the first formation, fold a cord and tie a stone chime knot (3). At the third side loop at top right, turn back the cord end and tie a cloverleaf knot with two outer loops (1) together with the second side loop. Repeat on the left (2), making sure both sides are identical. Continue downward, tying a double connection knot (4), a cloverleaf knot (5) and a button tassel (6). Insert beads in the two side loops of cloverleaf knot 5.

To make the second formation, fold a cord and tie a *pan chang* knot (7) followed by a round brocade knot with fourteen outer loops (14). Extend the second and sixth outer loops on the right into a cloverleaf knot (8, 10) and extend the fourth outer loop into a *pan chang* knot (9). Repeat on the left (11–13). On completing round brocade knot 14, tie a *pan chang* knot (15) and a button tassel (16). Insert beads in the center and in every second loop of round brocade knot 14. Fold two colored cords over each end of the belt and and sew them to the two knot formations. Tie button knots (17, 18) to hide the joins.

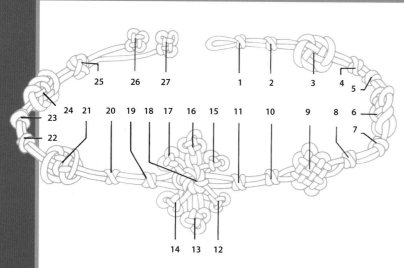

81 Fold a cord, leaving a small loop, then tie two double connection knots (1, 2), followed by a plafond knot (3) (see *Chinese Knotting*, page 56). Then, in sequence, tie two double connection knots (4, 5), a flat knot (6) (see *Chinese Knotting*, page 58), two double connection knots (7, 8), a *pan chang* knot (9), two double connection knots (10, 11) and a round brocade knot with six outer loops (18). Extend the first and third outer loops on the right side of the round brocade knot into a cloverleaf knot with two outer loops (12, 14), and extend the second outer loop into a cloverleaf knot (13). Repeat the steps (15–17) on the left side of round brocade knot 18. After completing the round brocade knot, tie two double connection knots (19, 20), a plafond knot (21), two double connection knots (22, 23) and a plafond knot (24). Then tie a button knot (25) to form a button to hook through the loop on the other end of the belt. Tie the remaining cord ends into cloverleaf knots (26, 27) and sew the ends inside the knot body.

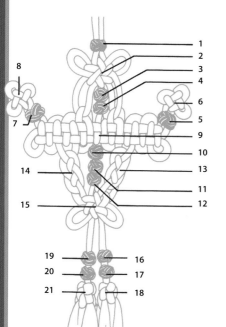

82 Fold a cord, tie a button ring knot (1) followed by a round brocade knot (2), lengthening its second outer loop on both sides. Pull both cord ends through two button ring knots (3, 4) and tie a long *pan chang* knot (9) (see *Chinese Knotting*, page 74). Hook up the first loop on the right side of the long *pan chang* knot with the lengthened outer loop of the round brocade knot above it. On completing the top right corner loop, tie a button ring knot (5) and extend it into a cloverleaf knot (6). On their way back, the cord ends must be pulled through the button ring knot again. Repeat the steps on the other side of the long *pan chang* knot (7, 8), making sure the left and right sides are identical. After completing the long *pan chang* knot, pull both cord ends through three button ring knots (10–12) and tie a round brocade knot (15). Tie the first outer loop on each side of the round brocade knot with the reserved side loops of the *pan chang* knot into a double coin knot (13, 14). On completing round brocade knot 15, pull each cord end through two button ring knots (16, 17; 19, 20) and tie two good luck tassels (18, 21).

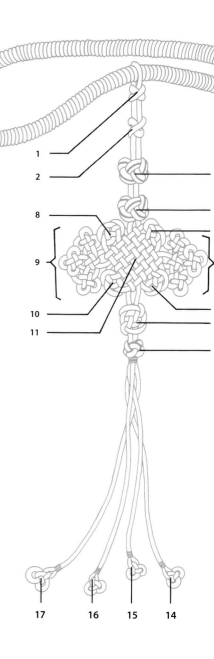

83 This belt comprises three knot formations. To make the first one, fold a cord and tie two double connection knots (1, 2) followed by two button ring knots (3, 4) and a *pan chang* knot (11). Tie the first and second loops on each side of the *pan chang* knot into a double coin knot (5, 7; 8, 10). Extend the corner loops on each side into a *ru yi* knot (6, 9). On completing the *pan chang* knot, continue downward, tying a plafond knot (12) (see *Chinese Knotting*, page 56) followed by a two-color button tassel (13). Tie the four cord ends of the tassel into cloverleaf knots and bind each with fine thread (14–17). The second knot formation is identical to the first except you need to tie an extra double connection knot at the beginning to make the two formations different lengths. The third knot formation – the belt – is made from a stiffer rope. Fold another cord, tie a button knot and wind the cord around the rope from end to end. Finally, fold the cord into a button receptacle.

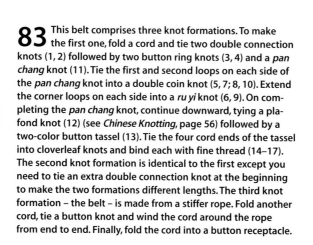

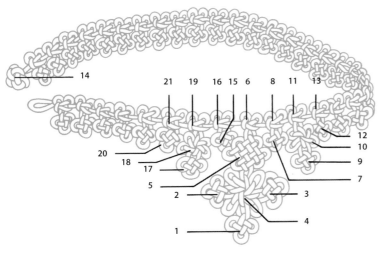

84 This belt is made from a single cord. Fold the cord into unequal lengths depending on the position of the hanging knot formation. Here, the left cord end is longer than the right one. Using the left cord end, start the tying process from the bottom part of the hanging knot formation. Tie a cloverleaf knot (1) followed by a round brocade knot with six outer loops (4) . Extend the middle outer loop on each side of the round brocade knot into a cloverleaf knot (2, 3). Then tie a *pan chang* knot (5) followed by a creeper knot (6). (Note that this knot formation hangs from the outer loop of creeper knot 6, which forms part of the belt.) Still using the longer left cord, tie another creeper knot (8) and extend its outer loop into a cloverleaf knot (7). Tie another creeper knot (11), extend its outer loop into a round brocade knot (10) and then extend the top outer loop into a cloverleaf knot (9). Then tie a long series of creeper knots and extend all their outer creeper loop into cloverleaf knots (13, 12). Apply the same tying technique to the shorter right cord end (15–20). Form a button knot (14) on the longer end of the belt and a loop on the shorter end.

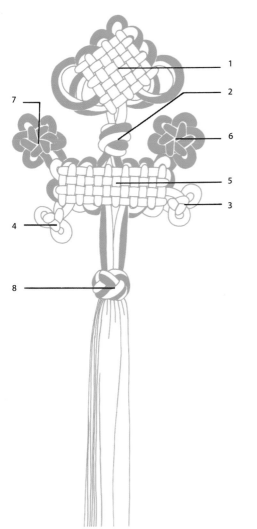

85 Use two different colored cords to make this eye-catching belt ornament. First, tie one cord into a multiple winged *pan chang* knot (1), then use the second cord to embellish its rim. Bring all four cord ends together and tie a double connection knot (2). Separate the first cord ends and use them to tie a long *pan chang* knot (5) (see *Chinese Knotting*, page 74). On completing the bottom corner loops on each side of the long *pan chang* knot, extend them into a cloverleaf knot with two outer loops (3, 4). Then, using the second cord ends, embellish the rim of the long *pan chang* knot, as shown at left, and extend the top corner loop on each side into a round brocade knot (6, 7). Bring all four cords together again and tie a button tassel (8) at a short distance below the long *pan chang* knot. The tassel cords can also be of two colors.

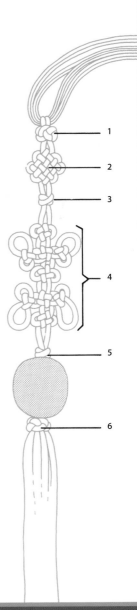

86 The two hanging knot formations on the ends of this belt are identical. To make each formation, fold a cord and, leaving a small loop at the top, tie a button knot (1), a *pan chang* knot (2), a double connection knot (3), a longevity knot (4) (see *Chinese Knotting*, page 64) and a double connection knot (5). Pull both cord ends through a porcelain bead (or any similar item) and tie a button tassel (6) below. Cords of similar colors can be used to make the tassel cords. To make the belt, string four cords of the same color through the loop above button knot 1 on the first knot formation, fold them and sew all eight cord ends onto button knot 1 of the second identical knot formation.

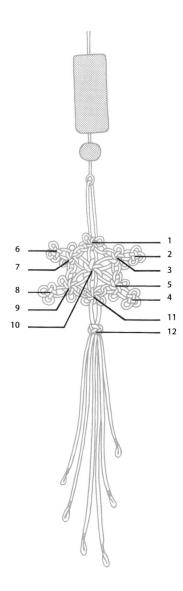

88 This elaborate belt decoration is made up of three separate knot formations hooked up as one. Its outer ring comprises six round brocade knots and six double coin knots; the inner ring, a cloverleaf knot with multiple outer loops; and the ring below, six cloverleaf knots. Starting from the top, fold a cord and tie two double connection knots (1, 2) followed by a round brocade knot (3) made with both cord ends. Lengthen the bottom left and right outer loops of round brocade knot 3 and tie a cloverleaf knot (4) in the inner ring. Then, separate the right cord end and tie it into a round brocade knot (6) at a suitable distance. Tie the outer loop of round brocade knot 6 with the adjoining outer loop of round brocade knot 3 into a double coin knot (5). Then tie a cloverleaf knot (7) just below round brocade knot 6 using the tying technique of the cloverleaf knot in the middle of the *ru yi* knot. Complete knots (8–16) following the same procedure, making sure the outer loops of all six cloverleaf knots in the inner ring are hooked up.

Using the connecting cords of the inner ring cloverleaf knots, tie the central cloverleaf knot with multiple outer loops (17). To complete the inner ring, tie the last cloverleaf knot (18) and hook up its outer loop with that of the adjoining cloverleaf knot 16. To complete the outer ring, tie the last round brocade knot (21). Tie its left and right outer loops with those of adjoining round brocade knots 9 and 15 into double coin knots (19, 20).

To make the last knot formation, at the bottom, first tie a double connection knot (22), then separate the right cord end to tie three cloverleaf knots (23–25) with two, three and two outer loops respectively. Do the same thing with the left cord end (26–28). Use the connecting cords of these six cloverleaf knots to tie a cloverleaf knot with multiple outer loops (29), followed by a double connection knot (30) just below it. Finally, tie a button tassel (31). Tie the remaining cord ends into cloverleaf knots (32–37) with two or three outer loops, turn back the ends and bind with fine thread.

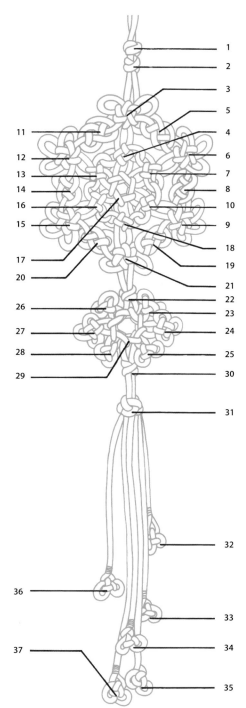

87 The ancient Chinese liked to hang a toothpick container on their belts for use as well as decoration. The design of this unique belt hanging, made up of eleven round brocade knots, is based on that concept. First, fold a cord through a toothpick container and tie a round brocade knot (1) followed by another round brocade knot (10). Extend the four outer loops of round brocade knot 10 into a round brocade knot (3, 5; 7, 9), then extend the outermost loop of each into a cloverleaf knot (2, 4; 6, 8). After completing round brocade knot 10, tie another round brocade knot (11). Finally, tie a button tassel (12). Fold back the cord ends and bind them with fine thread.

BRACELETS

See page 48 for photographs of applications 89–94.

89 Tie a copper wire into a series of flat button knots and hook up the two ends to form a bracelet.

90 To make this bracelet, first cross two strands of double cords, then tie a four-layer good luck tassel head. Fix a button ring knot made of gold cord to the four cord ends. Repeat the process of tying a good luck tassel head and fixing a gold cord button ring knot until the desired length for the bracelet is reached, then join both ends with a metallic knot and hook.

91 Tie a cord into a series of flat button knots to form this bracelet. Hook up all the button knots with a gold cord, then sew a metallic hook and knot on the ends of the bracelet.

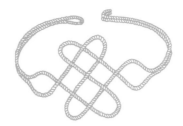

92 This upper arm ring is made from a length of metallic cord with a slanted grain. Fold the cord in half and leave a small loop at one end of the ring. Unite the two ends of the folded cord below the loop and leave enough length for the lower circumference of the arm. Since metallic cords are stiff and not easily distorted, bend both sides of the folded cord into a simple *pan chang* knot shape, as shown above. Unite the cord ends and wrap around half the circumference of the upper arm. Bend the cord ends into a hook for attaching to the loop. Before making this upper arm ring, do a drawing to determine the length required as excessive bending might make the cord snap. If you use pliers instead of your hands to bend the cord, be careful not to crack the cord.

93 Gloves can be decorated with knot formations for added elegance. Fold a cord and tie a cloverleaf knot (1) followed by a round brocade knot with six outer loops (4). Extend the middle outer loop on each side of the round brocade knot into a cloverleaf knot (2, 3). On completing the round brocade knot, tie a double connection knot (5) and a cloverleaf knot (6) followed by a *hui ling* knot (9). Tie the side loops just before and after the right corner loops of the *hui ling* knot into a cloverleaf knot (7, 8), making sure the left and right sides of the knot are identical. On completing the *hui ling* knot, separate the cord ends and tie a cloverleaf knot on each (10, 11), then bring them together to tie a cloverleaf knot (12). Tie a second group of three cloverleaf knots (13–15) following

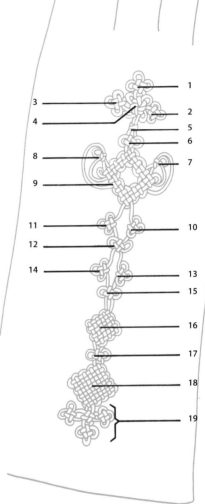

steps 10–12. Then tie a *pan chang* knot (16), a cloverleaf knot (17) and a *pan chang* knot (18). On completing the *pan chang* knot, hide one cord end inside the knot body. Tie the other cord end into a *ru yi* knot (19) and hide it also inside the *pan chang* knot body. Finally, sew the knot formation onto the glove.

94 This bracelet is made with a silver guitar string. Fold the string, then twist the fold to form a loop. Bind the twisted cord end with thread. Tie a series of double connection knots until the desired length is reached, then bend the end of the string into a hook and bind with thread. Attach love beans to the middle of each double connection knot with strong glue.

RINGS

See page 49 for photographs of applications 95–97.

95 This ring is made from thick fuse wire. Fold and twist a piece of wire long enough to wrap around the finger – or the wrist, for a bracelet. Tie the ends into a round brocade knot. After gold-plating the wire, insert porcelain beads in the outer loops with strong glue.

96 This ring is made from two thin plastic straws. Use a pencil or some other cylindrical shape for the axis. Wrap one of the plastic straws around the axis and tie a button ring knot. Use the other straw to tie another round following the original weave. Cut the straw ends just inside the ring.

97 This ring is made from a silver guitar string. Tie a flat button knot. Wrap each cord end once around the finger and leave a suitable length for the ring. Insert one cord end into the back of the knot body. Weave the other cord end around the button knot and then insert it also into the back of the knot body.

FOOTWEAR ACCENTS

See page 50 for photographs of applications 98–102.

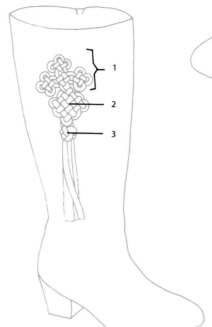

98 Knot formations made from leather cord can add glamour to boots. With the leather side facing out, tie a *ru yi* knot (1), a *pan chang* knot (2) and a button tassel (3). Use strong glue to attach the knot formation to the boot.

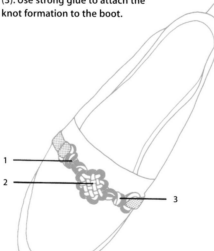

101 This knot formation can be used to link two rings on the sides of a shoe. Insert a cord through one of the rings and tie a double connection knot (1). Insert one of the cord ends through the other ring and tie a double connection knot (3). Bring the cord ends to the middle. Tie one into a *pan chang* knot (2) and use the other to embellish its rim. Unite the cord ends, trim off excess and glue under the knot formation.

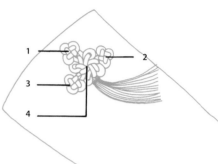

99 Tie a leather cord into a round brocade knot. Tie the ends and hide them in the body of the knot. Use strong glue to attach the knot to the top of the shoe.

100 Fold a multicolored cord and tie a cloverleaf knot (1) followed by a round brocade knot with six outer loops (2). Extend the middle outer loops on each side into a cloverleaf knot (3, 4). Bind the cord ends with thread near the knot body, then brush out the ends to make a tassel. Pin the knot formation to the sock.

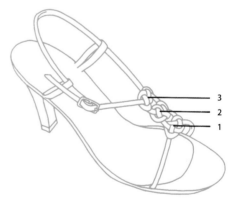

102 Any number of knot formations can be tied to make customized high heel shoes or sandals. This knot formation comprises three double connection knots (1–3) tied with a leather cord, with plenty of cord end left for making the other shoe straps. The finished knot formation and extra leather cord will have to be passed to a shoe shop for attaching to the buckle and the sole.

OTHER DECORATIONS See pages 51–54 for photographs of applications 103–123.

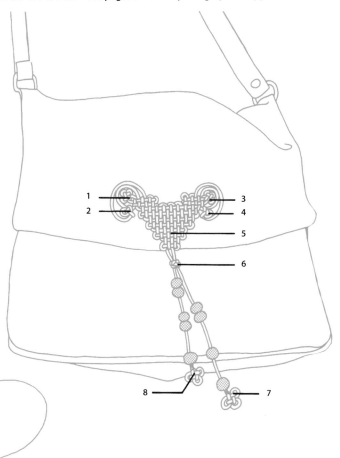

103 Knot formations can enliven plain shoulder bags. For this decorative knot, first tie a golden bell knot (5), then extend its bottom right corner loop into a cloverleaf knot (1). Tie the side loops immediately to the right and left of the corner loop into a cloverleaf knot with two outer loops (2). Repeat the steps for the left side (3, 4), making sure both sides are identical. On completing the golden bell knot, pull both cord ends through the knot body and out through the top, then tie them into a button knot (6). String each cord end with some colored beads. Then tie each cord end into a cloverleaf knot (7, 8). Fold the cord ends back and bind with fine thread. Use strong glue to attach the knot formation to the bag.

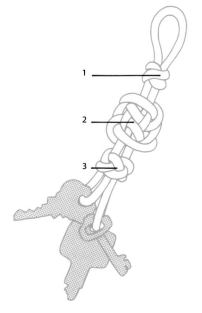

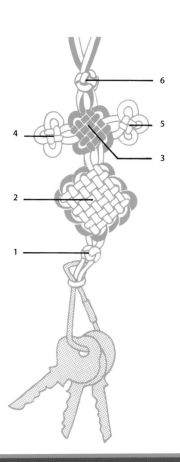

104 To make this key ring, fold a leather cord with its leather side facing out and leave a small loop at the top for hanging the keys. Then tie a double connection knot (1), a plafond knot (2) (see *Chinese Knotting*, page 56) and a button knot (3). Pull both cord ends through the keys, as shown, and hide them inside the body of the button knot. Since the leather surface is quite rough, the cord ends will not slide out. Whenever more keys need to be added, pull out the cord ends, restring the keys, then hide the ends back inside the body of the button knot.

105 For the key chain on the right, fold a plastic cord through the key ring and tie a button knot (1) followed by a *pan chang* knot (2). Use another cord to embellish the rim of the *pan chang* knot, then tie a smaller *pan chang* knot (3) just below the first one with the same cord. Pull the cord ends of *pan chang* knot 2 through the body of *pan chang* knot 3 and extend them into a cloverleaf knot (4, 5) on the corner loop on each side. Pull the cord ends out through the knot body of *pan chang* knot 3. Finally, tie all four cord ends into a button tassel (6).

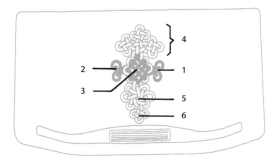

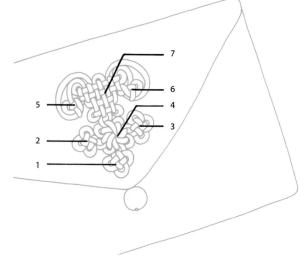

106 The knot formation on this leather handbag is made with two leather cords with their leather sides facing out. Tie the first leather cord into a *pan chang* knot (3) and extend the corner loop on each side into a cloverleaf knot (1, 2). Hide both cord ends inside the knot body. Fold the second leather cord and tie a *ru yi* knot (4). Use both cord ends of the *ru yi* knot to embellish the rim of the *pan chang* knot, then tie a round brocade knot with six outer loops (5) beneath it. Sew one cord end into the knot body. Tie the other one into a cloverleaf knot (6), then sew it also into the knot body. Use strong glue to attach the knot formation to the handbag.

107 Fold a cord and tie a cloverleaf knot (1) followed by a round brocade knot with six outer loops (4). Extend the middle outer loop on each side of the round brocade knot into a cloverleaf knot (2, 3). On completing the round brocade knot, tie both cord ends into a *san cai* knot (7). Tie the side loop on each side of the bottom right outer loop of the *san cai* knot into a cloverleaf knot (5, 6). Make sure the left and right sides are identical. On completing the *san cai* knot, hide both cord ends inside the knot body and sew or glue the knot formation onto the leather bag, as shown. Sew a porcelain bead at the bottom of the knot formation to weigh down the front flap of the bag so that it closes tightly.

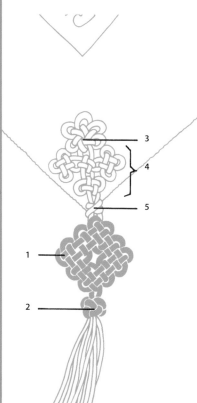

108 Fold a cord and tie a *hui ling* knot (1) followed by a button tassel (2). Fold another cord and tie a round brocade knot (3), an inverted *ru yi* knot (4) and a double connection knot (5). Hide the cord ends inside the body of the *hui ling* knot. Sew the knot formation onto one corner of the scarf.

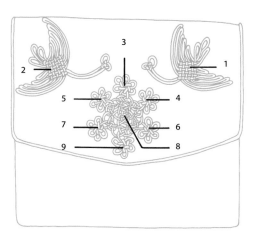

109 A golden knot formation adds sophistication to a brown velvet handbag (or any other type of bag). First, tie two crane knots (1, 2) (see *Chinese Knotting*, page 80) and sew them onto the top left and right sides of the bag flap. Then fold a gold cord and tie a round brocade knot (3). Tie both cord ends into a six unity knot (8) and extend the two double connection knots on each side into a round brocade knot (4–6). On completing the six unity knot, tie both cord ends into a round brocade knot (9). Hide one cord end inside the knot body. Tie the other into a loop and sew it onto the knot body. Finally, sew this knot formation onto the handbag.

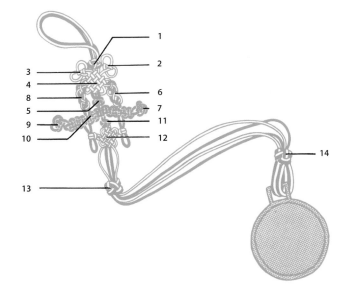

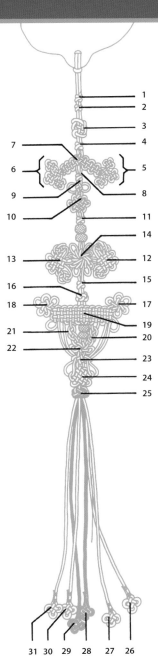

110 This is an ornament for hanging on the rod supporting the bottom of a Chinese painting or scroll. Fold a cord and tie a button knot (1). String it with a small crystal (or other bead) and tie a cloverleaf knot (2) followed by a round brocade knot with six outer loops (5). Extend the middle outer loop on each side of the round brocade knot into a cloverleaf knot (3, 4). Finally, tie a button tassel (6), bind the tassel head with fine thread and sew beads into the loops.

111 Fold a cord and tie two double connection knots (1, 2) followed by a plafond knot (3) (see *Chinese Knotting*, page 56) and a double connection knot (4). Then tie a stone chime knot (7) and extend each side of the knot into a *ru yi* knot (5, 6). Bring the cord ends together below the stone chime knot and tie them into a double connection knot (8), a cloverleaf knot (9), a *pan chang* knot (10) and a double connection knot (11). String two porcelain beads, then tie a round brocade knot with ten outer loops (14). Extend the middle outer loop on each side into a butterfly knot (12, 13). At the bottom of round brocade knot 14, tie both cord ends into a double connection knot (15) and a button knot (16). Then tie a long *pan chang* knot (19) (see *Chinese Knotting*, page 74). Extend the top right corner loop of the long *pan chang* knot into a round brocade knot (17). On completing the bottom right corner loop, pull it out. When the first and third loops on the bottom right side are done, leave a suitable length of cord. Repeat the steps on the left side of the *pan chang* knot (18), making sure that both sides are identical. When *pan chang* knot 19 is completed, string both cord ends with two porcelain beads and tie them into a round brocade knot (22). Tie the first outer loop on each side of the knot with the third bottom side loop on each side of the *pan chang* knot into a double coin knot (20, 21). Continue down, tying a cloverleaf knot (23) and a *pan chang* knot (24). Pull the lengthened bottom first side loop on each side of long *pan chang* knot 19 through the two outer loops of cloverleaf knot 23, then hook them up with the corner loop on each side of *pan chang* knot 24. Finally, tie a two-color button tassel (25). Tie all six cord ends into a cloverleaf knot (26–31) and bind each end with fine thread.

112 To make this pocket watch decoration, first fold two plastic cords and tie a button knot (1). Use one cord to tie a *pan chang* knot (4), then extend the top loop on each side into a cloverleaf knot with two outer loops (2, 3). Leave a suitable length on the bottom corner loops of *pan chang* knot 4. Pull the second cord through the body of *pan chang* knot 4 and tie a button knot (5) followed by a long *pan chang* knot (10) (see *Chinese Knotting*, page 74). Using the tying technique of the double coin knot, hook up one of the top side loops on each side of long *pan chang* knot 10 with the corner loop on each side of *pan chang* knot 4 (6, 8), then extend the the corner loop on each side into a double coin knot (7, 9). Leave a suitable length on one of the bottom loops on each side of long *pan chang* knot 10. Then pull the cord ends of *pan chang* knot 4 through the knot bodies of button knot 5 and *pan chang* knot 10 and tie a button knot (11) followed by a *pan chang* knot (12). Hook up the corner loop on each side of *pan chang* knot 12 with the extended bottom loops of long *pan chang* knot 10. Then tie the four cord ends into two interspaced button knots (13, 14). Pull the cord ends through the hook on the pocket watch and sew them inside the knot body.

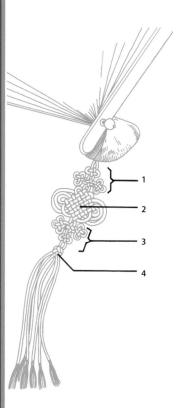

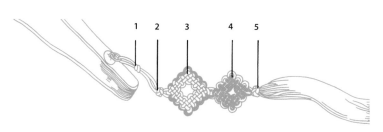

114 For this fan decoration, fold a cord through the small hole at the bottom of the fan and tie a double connection knot (1), a button knot (2) and a *hui ling* knot (3). Embellish the rim of the *hui ling* knot with another cord (see page 17 above). Then tie a small *hui ling* knot (4) using the second cord. Hide both cord ends inside the knot body. Using the two original cord ends, embellish the rim of the second *hui ling* knot. Finally, tie a button tassel (5).

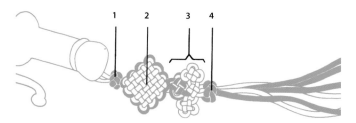

113 To make this hanging ornament for a sandalwood (or other) fan, first pull a cord through the hole at the bottom of the fan, then fold it and tie a *ru yi* knot (1), a winged *pan chang* knot (2) and a *ru yi* knot (3). Finally, tie a button tassel (4). Fasten the cord ends of the tassel with silver threads, as shown above.

115 Use plastic cords that are heat and water resistant to tie this knot formation for the handlebars of a bicycle. Fold a cord and tie a button knot (1), a *pan chang* knot (2), a *ru yi* knot (3) and a button tassel (4). Take two other cords and weave them separately through the button knot and the button tassel to give two colors. Embellish the rim of the *pan chang* knot with another cord, and weave both cord ends into the cloverleaf knot on the top part of the *ru yi* knot to make it a two-color cloverleaf knot. Fold and sew two other cords onto the button tassel to add more color (see page 112 above).

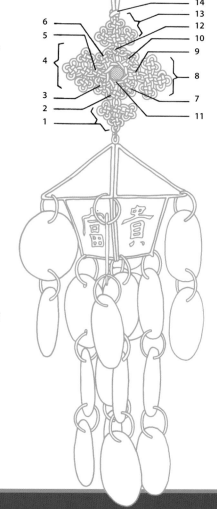

116 Fold a cord through the loop at the top of this Filipino wind chime made from seashells and tie a *ru yi* knot (1) followed by a cloverleaf knot (2). Separate the right cord and tie a cloverleaf knot (3), hooking its middle outer loop to the adjacent loop of cloverleaf knot 2. Then tie a *ru yi* knot (4) followed by another cloverleaf knot (5). Make sure cloverleaf knot 5 is hooked up with the outer loop of cloverleaf knot 3. Tie another cloverleaf knot (6) whose outer loop is hooked up with cloverleaf knot 5. Repeat the steps on the left side (7–10), making sure both sides are identical. Bring together the cord ends of this group of cloverleaf knots and tie a cloverleaf knot with multiple outer loops (11). Then tie both cord ends into a cloverleaf knot (12) and hook them up with the outer loops of cloverleaf knots 6 and 10. Finally, tie an inverted *ru yi* knot (13) followed by a double connection knot (14). Leave enough cord at the end for hanging the wind chime. Sew a cultured pearl (or other bead) in the center of the knot formation.

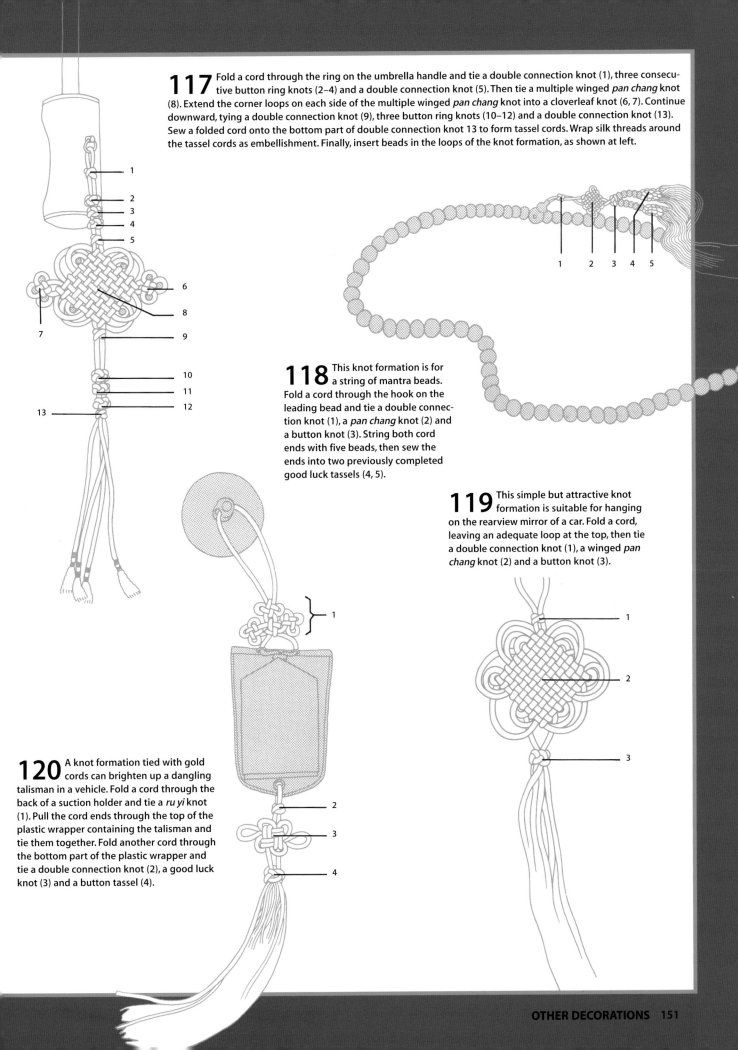

117 Fold a cord through the ring on the umbrella handle and tie a double connection knot (1), three consecutive button ring knots (2–4) and a double connection knot (5). Then tie a multiple winged *pan chang* knot (8). Extend the corner loops on each side of the multiple winged *pan chang* knot into a cloverleaf knot (6, 7). Continue downward, tying a double connection knot (9), three button ring knots (10–12) and a double connection knot (13). Sew a folded cord onto the bottom part of double connection knot 13 to form tassel cords. Wrap silk threads around the tassel cords as embellishment. Finally, insert beads in the loops of the knot formation, as shown at left.

118 This knot formation is for a string of mantra beads. Fold a cord through the hook on the leading bead and tie a double connection knot (1), a *pan chang* knot (2) and a button knot (3). String both cord ends with five beads, then sew the ends into two previously completed good luck tassels (4, 5).

119 This simple but attractive knot formation is suitable for hanging on the rearview mirror of a car. Fold a cord, leaving an adequate loop at the top, then tie a double connection knot (1), a winged *pan chang* knot (2) and a button knot (3).

120 A knot formation tied with gold cords can brighten up a dangling talisman in a vehicle. Fold a cord through the back of a suction holder and tie a *ru yi* knot (1). Pull the cord ends through the top of the plastic wrapper containing the talisman and tie them together. Fold another cord through the bottom part of the plastic wrapper and tie a double connection knot (2), a good luck knot (3) and a button tassel (4).

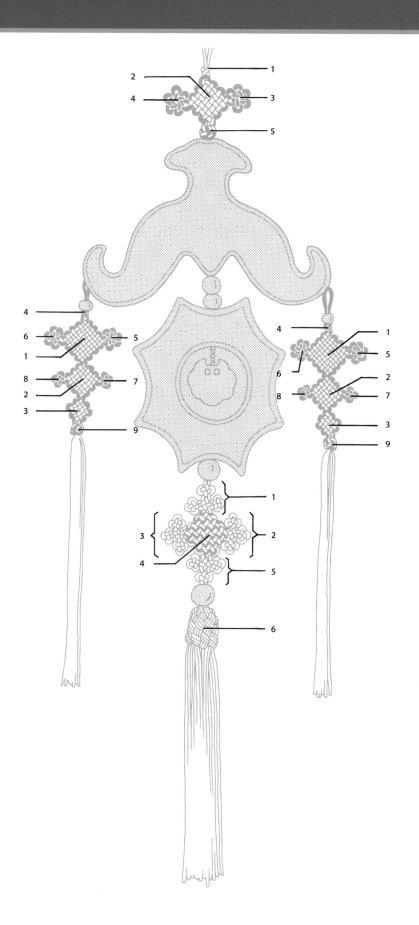

121 This hanging ornament, comprising four separate knot formations, denotes prosperity and longevity. To make the top knot formation, fold a cord and tie a double connection knot (1), a *pan chang* knot (2) and a button knot (5). Embellish the rim of the *pan chang* knot with another cord, at the same time extending the corner loop on each side into a round brocade knot (3, 4). Weave the cord ends into the button knot and sew them inside the knot body.

The tying technique for the knot formation on the left and right is exactly the same. Fold a cord and tie a big (1), medium (2) and small (3) *pan chang* knot followed by a button knot (9). Fold another cord and string it with a multicolored (or other) porcelain bead, leaving a small loop at the top. Tie a double connection knot (4), then embellish the rims of the three *pan chang* knots with the cord. Using the same cord, extend the corner loop on each side of big *pan chang* knot 1 into a round brocade knot (5, 6). Extend the corner loop on each side of medium *pan chang* knot 2 into a cloverleaf knot (7, 8). After completing the rim embellishment on small *pan chang* knot 3, tie both cord ends into a button knot (9), then sew them inside the knot body. Sew a bundle of cords onto the button knot to form tassel cords.

The name of the bottom knot formation is "Happiness in the Four Seasons." Fold a cord, string it with a porcelain (or other) bead and tie a *ru yi* knot (1) followed by a *pan chang* knot (4). Extend the corner loops on each side of the *pan chang* knot into a *ru yi* knot (2, 3). Do not tighten the *pan chang* knot yet. Weave a gold cord alongside the original cord of the *pan chang* knot, then only tighten the knot. Sew both ends of the gold cord and one end of the original cord inside the knot body. Tie the other one into a *ru yi* knot (5), then sew it also inside the knot body. Sew a porcelain bead with a diagonal weave tassel (6) onto the bottom of the knot formation. After completing all four knot formations, sew them onto the hanging pendant, as shown at left.

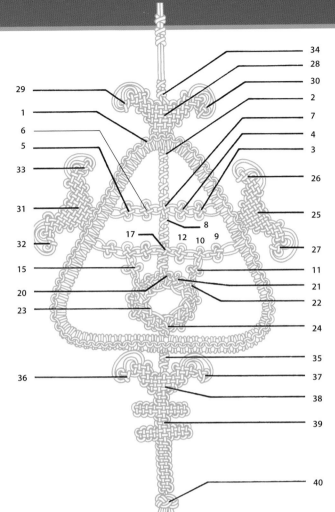

Repeat steps 9–12 with the left cord (13–16), extending the bottom outer loop of middle cloverleaf knot 14 into another cloverleaf knot (15). Then tie a cloverleaf knot (17) using the tying technique of cloverleaf knot 7 above to complete the second horizontal stroke of *ji*. Tie another two double connection knots (18, 19) followed by a cloverleaf knot (20). Separate the right cord, tie five cloverleaf knots (21), hooking up their adjacent outer loops. The top outer loop of cloverleaf knot (22) should be hooked up with cloverleaf knot 11. Do exactly the same for the left cord end. Use the connecting cords from this group of cloverleaf knots to tie a cloverleaf knot with multiple outer loops (23) followed by another cloverleaf knot (24). Hook up the outer loops on both sides of cloverleaf knot 24 with the adjacent cloverleaf knots. Hide both cord ends inside the body of the flat knots on the frame, thus completing the character *ji*.

To make the second part of the formation, use three new cords to tie three modified golden bell knots outside the frame – one on the right (25), one on the top (28) and one on the left (31). The top part of each golden bell knot must be hooked up with the frame, as shown. For each golden bell knot, extend the left and right corner loops into a cloverleaf knot with two outer loops (26, 27; 29, 30; 32, 33). After completing the golden bell knots, sew the cord ends inside the knot body, except that of golden bell knot 28, which must be tied into four groups of interspaced double connection knots (34) for hanging. The number of double connection knots in the four groups (not all are shown) are two, three, four and five respectively. Finally, bind the cord ends with fine thread.

The third formation at the bottom (the Chinese character *yang*) comprises a modified golden bell knot and a double ten knot. Fold a cord through the central flat knot on the bottom of the frame and tie two double connection knots (35). Lengthen both cord ends and tie a double ten knot (39) to complete the bottom part of *yang*. Then tie both cord ends into a modified golden bell knot (38) with the left and right corner loops extended into a cloverleaf knot with two outer loops (36, 37) as per the tying technique of knots 29 and 30 above. This completes the top part of *yang.* Attach a button tassel (40) to the bottom part of *yang* to finish off the hanging ornament.

122 This knot formation, symbolizing "The Three Rams That Bring Good Luck and Fortune," comprises three parts: the Chinese character *ji* (meaning good luck) inside the frame; three modified golden bell knots attached to the outside of the frame; and the Chinese character *yang* (meaning ram) just below the frame. First, wrap a rattan frame with a cord using the tying technique of the flat knot (1) (see *Chinese Knotting*, page 58). Then fold a cord through the flat knot on the top corner of the frame and tie five consecutive double connection knots (2). Separate the right cord, leave a suitable length and tie a cloverleaf knot (3), hooking its outer loop to the flat knot on the frame. Then tie another cloverleaf knot (4). Repeat steps 3 and 4 with the left cord (5, 6). Tie a cloverleaf knot (7) with the two cords using the tying technique of the middle cloverleaf knot within the *ru yi* knot. The first horizontal stroke of *ji* has thus been completed. Continue downward, tying three double connection knots (8). Separate the right cord and tie three cloverleaf knots (9, 10, 12) in the same way as cloverleaf knots 3 and 4 above, hooking the outer loop of cloverleaf knot 9 to the flat knot on the frame. Extend the bottom outer loop of cloverleaf knot 10 into another cloverleaf knot (11).

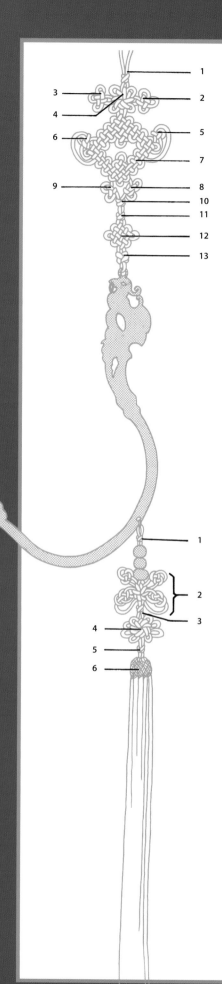

123 These two knot formations add both elegance and glamour to a mosquito net hook. To make the top knot formation, fold a cord and tie a double connection knot (1) followed by a round brocade knot with six outer loops (4). Extend the middle outer loop on each side of the round brocade knot into a cloverleaf knot (2, 3). On completing the round brocade knot, tie both cord ends into a special knot (7) that half resembles a crossed *hui ling* knot and half resembles a *hui ling* knot; that is, its top and bottom internal corners are tied using the technique of a crossed *hui ling* knot, but the left and right internal corners use the technique of a *hui ling* knot. After making the body of special knot 7, tie the first corner loop on both sides into a cloverleaf knot (5, 6). After completing knot 7, tie each cord end separately into a cloverleaf knot with two outer loops (8, 9). Bring the cord ends together and tie two double connection knots (10, 11), a *pan chang* knot (12) and a button knot (13). Finally, pull both cord ends through the ring on top of the mosquito net hook and sew them inside the knot body.

To make the bottom knot formation, fold a cord through the hole in the bottom part of the mosquito net hook, tie a double connection knot (1), then string three porcelain (or other) beads on the cords. Tie a round brocade knot with six outer loops (2). Extend each of the three outer loops on both sides of the knot into a double coin knot, making sure that the left and right sides are identical. After completing the butterfly-shaped round brocade knot, tie both cord ends into a double connection knot (3) followed by a round brocade knot with eight outer loops (4) and another double connection knot (5). Complete this second formation by sewing on a diagonal weave tassel (6).

See pages 8–24 for photographs of applications 124–135 below.

124 This hanging pendant (see photograph page 11) comprises five knot formations. To make the top knot formation, fold a cord and tie a button knot (1), a plafond knot (2) (see *Chinese Knotting*, page 56) and another button knot (3).

To make the knot formation in the center, fold a cord and tie an inverted *ru yi* knot (1), a button knot (2) and a *ru yi* knot (3). Enhance the button knot by binding the cords just above and below it with fine threads.

The knot formation on the left and right of the pendant is identical. To make it, fold a cord and tie a cloverleaf knot (1) followed by a *hui ling* knot (4). Extend the left and right corner loops of the *hui ling* knot into a cloverleaf knot (2, 3). Then use another cord to embellish the top left and right rims of the *hui ling* knot. On reaching cloverleaf knots 2 and 3 at the sides, pull the ends of this second cord through the body of the *hui ling* knot and into the central space. Tie four interlinking cloverleaf knots (5–8). Continue to embellish the bottom left and right rims of the *hui ling* knot with the second cord, then hide the cord ends inside the knot body. Tie the original cord ends into a cloverleaf knot (9) and three double connection knots (10–12). Finally, sew a diagonal weave tassel (13) on the bottom of the formation.

To make the bottom knot formation, fold a cord and tie a *ru yi* knot (1) followed by a *pan chang* knot (8). Extend the loops on each corner of the *pan chang* knot into a cloverleaf knot (4–7), then lengthen the bottom outer loops of cloverleaf knots 5 and 7. Do not tighten the *pan chang* knot body yet. Weave another cord into the *pan chang* knot along the right side of the original cord, and extend it into a cloverleaf knot (2). Repeat on the left side to create cloverleaf (3). Tighten the *pan chang* knot and hide the ends of the second cord inside the knot body. String a porcelain bead on the original cord ends. Tie the right cord, together with the bottom outer loop of cloverleaf knot 2, into another cloverleaf knot (9). Then tie the same cord end, together with the bottom outer loop of cloverleaf knot 9, into a cloverleaf knot with two outer loops (10). Do exactly the same thing with the left cord end to form cloverleaf knots (11) and (12). Bring both cord ends together and tie a cloverleaf knot (13) using the tying technique of the cloverleaf knot in the middle of the *ru yi* knot. Then tie a plafond knot (14) and two double connection knots (15, 16). Finally, sew a diagonal weave tassel (17) onto the bottom of the formation.

Sew all five knot formations onto the pendant, as shown at right.

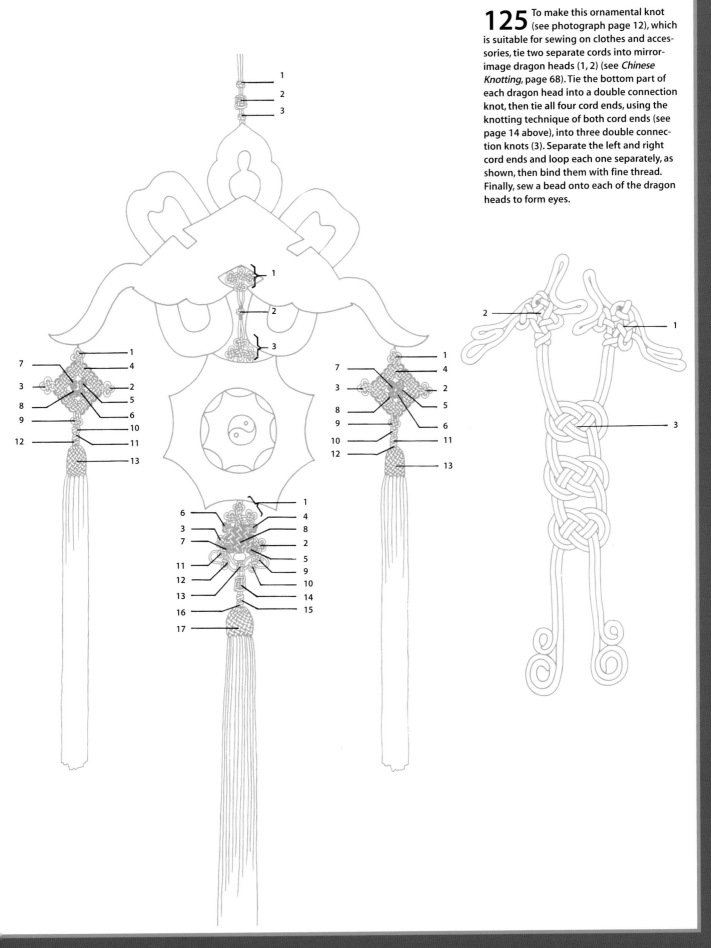

125 To make this ornamental knot (see photograph page 12), which is suitable for sewing on clothes and accessories, tie two separate cords into mirror-image dragon heads (1, 2) (see *Chinese Knotting*, page 68). Tie the bottom part of each dragon head into a double connection knot, then tie all four cord ends, using the knotting technique of both cord ends (see page 14 above), into three double connection knots (3). Separate the left and right cord ends and loop each one separately, as shown, then bind them with fine thread. Finally, sew a bead onto each of the dragon heads to form eyes.

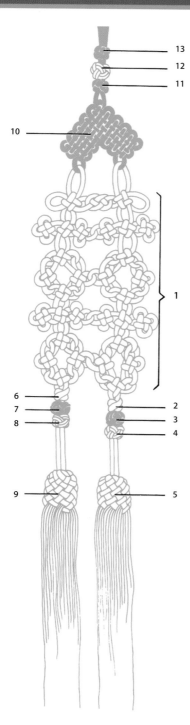

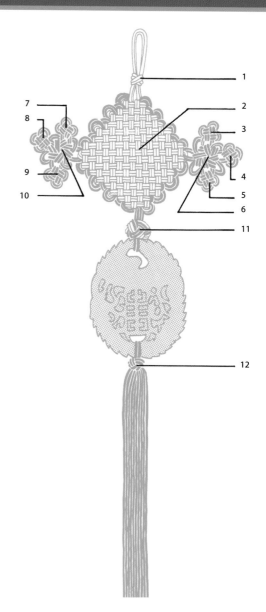

126 To make this dangling ornament (see photograph page 14), tie two cords into a double happiness knot (1) (see *Chinese Knotting*, page 66), but do not directly hook up the first horizontal stroke. Instead, hook it up with a double coin knot. After completing the double happiness knot, tie the two cord ends on the right side into a double connection knot (2) followed by two button ring knots (3, 4). Sew a diagonal weave tassel (5) on the bottom. Repeat the steps for the left side (6–9). Fold another cord and tie a stone chime knot (10). Hook up the bottom corner loops on each side with double happiness knot 1. After completing the stone chime knot, pull both cord ends through the body of the knot and out the top and tie a button knot (11), a button ring knot (12), another button knot (13), and (not shown) a plafond knot (see *Chinese Knotting*, page 56) and double connection knot for hanging.

127 The cord material for this knot formation (see photograph page 15) is called "snake's abdomen." Since the cord looks like two conjoined cords, the resulting knot formation is very unusual. Fold a snake abdomen cord and tie a double connection knot (1) followed by a *ling hua* knot (2). Fold another cord and embellish the rim of the *ling hua* knot. Extend the corner loop on each side of the *ling hua* knot into a round brocade knot with six outer loops (6, 10). Extend every other outer loop into a cloverleaf (3–5; 7–9). Bring the four cord ends together at the bottom of the *ling hua* knot and tie them into a button knot (11). Hide three cord ends inside the knot body and pull the remaining one through the piece of jade (or other ornamental object). Make a separate button tassel (12) and tie it to the cord end at the bottom of the jade piece.

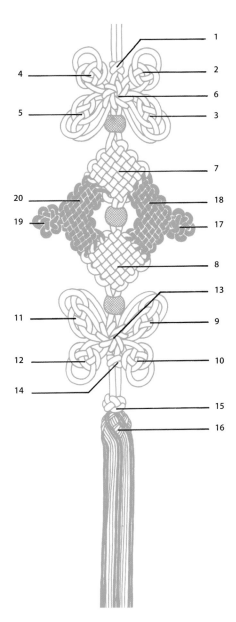

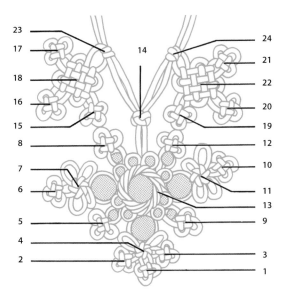

129 To make this interesting necklace (see photograph page 13), fold a cord and tie a cloverleaf knot (1) followed by a round brocade knot (4). Extend the first outer loop on each side into a cloverleaf knot (2, 3). Then tie a round brocade knot with fourteen outer loops (13). Extend the second and sixth outer loops on the right side of the round brocade knot into a cloverleaf knot (9, 12). Extend the fourth outer loop into a round brocade knot (11) and extend its outermost loop into a cloverleaf knot (10). Repeat on the left side of the knot formation (5–8), making sure the left and right sides are identical. After completing the fourteen-loop round brocade knot, bring together both cords and tie a button knot (14). Then separate the cords and tie each one into a *pan chang* knot (18, 22). Extend the top, left and right corner loops of both *pan chang* knots into a cloverleaf knot (15–17; 19–21). Fold another cord and sew it into the body of button knot 14, then separate the cord ends and separately tie a simple knot (23, 24) at the bottom part of each *pan chang* knot. Continue tying a series of interspaced simple knots on both cords to prevent them from going slack. Tie one end of the necklace cord into a button knot and the other into a loop. Sew together the adjacent outer loops of cloverleaf knots 8 and 15, 12 and 19 to hold the knot formation in place. Finally, sew beads of different sizes into the loops of the knot formation, as shown above.

128 To make this dangling ornament (see photograph page 17), fold a cord and tie a double connection knot (1) followed by a round brocade knot with six outer loops (6). Extend the first outer loop on each side of the round brocade knot into a double connection knot (2, 4). Tie the second and third outer loops together into a double connection knot (3, 5). Make sure the left and right sides are identical and are shaped like an inverted butterfly. Bring the cord ends together and string a porcelain (or other) bead, then tie a *pan chang* knot (7). String another bead and tie another *pan chang* knot (8). String a third bead, then tie a butterfly-shaped knot formation (9–13), which is a mirror image of the inverted butterfly completed in steps 2–6. Continue downward, tying a double connection knot (14) followed by a button knot (15). Sew a two-color button tassel (16) onto it. Then tie two cords separately into a round brocade knot (17), a stone chime knot (18), a round brocade knot (19) and a stone chime knot (20). Hook up the bottom side loops on each side of stone chime knots 18 and 20 with the outer loops of *pan chang* knots 7 and 8, as shown above.

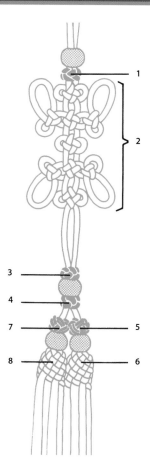

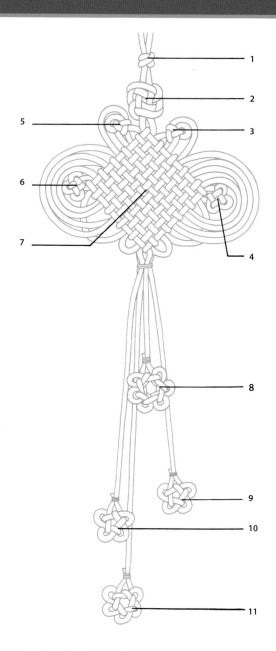

130 To make this hanging ornamental knot formation (see photograph page 18), fold a cord, string the cord ends with a porcelain (or other) bead, then tie a button ring knot (1) followed by a longevity knot (2) (see *Chinese Knotting*, page 64). Leave a suitable length of cord, then tie another button ring knot (3). String the cord ends with a second porcelain (or other) bead, then tie a third button ring knot (4). Separate the cord ends and on each tie a button ring knot (5, 7). Finally, string a porcelain bead on each and attach a diagonal weave tassel (6, 8).

131 For this striking knot formation (see photograph page 19), fold a cord and tie a double connection knot (1), a plafond knot (2) (see *Chinese Knotting*, page 56) and a winged *pan chang* knot (7). Tie the first and second side loops on the top right of the winged *pan chang* knot into a cloverleaf knot with two outer loops (3) and extend the right corner loop into a cloverleaf knot (4). Repeat on the left side (5, 6), making sure both sides are identical. After completing the winged *pan chang* knot, hook another cord to the bottom of it. Tie each of the four cord ends into a cloverleaf knot with four (9, 10), five (11) and six (8) outer loops. Then bind all four cord ends with fine gold thread as well as the four cords just beneath the winged *pan chang* knot.

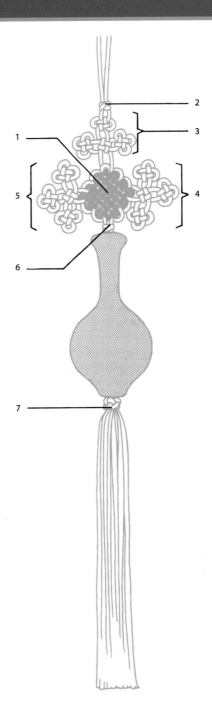

132 A knotted phoenix (see photograph page 20) makes a delightful decoration on clothes, accessories and soft furnishings. To make the phoenix knot, see *Chinese Knotting*, page 82. After completing the phoenix knot, embellish it with another cord of a similar color, as shown above, to enhance its beauty.

133 This necklace is best made in colors that complement those of the porcelain vase included in the knot formation (see photograph page 22). To make the formation, fold a cord, tie a *pan chang* knot (1), then hide the ends of the cord inside the body of the knot. Take another cord, leave enough length for the necklace loop, then tie a double connection knot (2) followed by a *ru yi* knot (3). Separate the two cord ends and use them to embellish the top left and right rims of the *pan chang* knot. When the cord ends reach the corner loops on each side of the *pan chang* knot, extend them into a *ru yi* knot (4, 5), then continue to embellish the bottom left and right rims of the *pan chang* knot. Bring the cords ends together and tie them into a double connection knot (6) just below the *pan chang* knot. Finally, pull both cord ends through the porcelain vase and tie a button tassel (7).

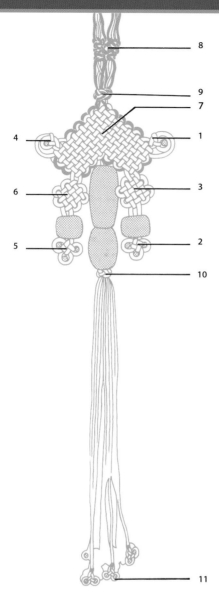

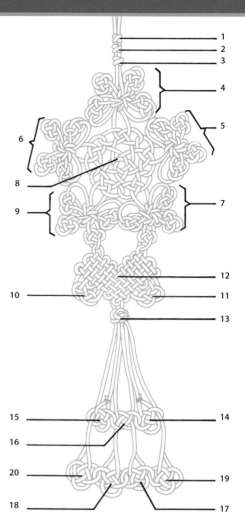

134 To make this hanging knot formation (see photograph page 23), fold a cord and tie a stone chime knot (7). On completing the top right corner loop, turn back the cord end and tie a cloverleaf knot with two outer loops (1) with the adjacent top right side loop. After finishing the bottom right corner loop, extend it into a *pan chang* knot (3). String the bottom corner loop on the *pan chang* knot with a bead, then extend it into a cloverleaf knot (2). Turn back the cord end, pull it through the bead again and complete *pan chang* knot 3. Repeat the steps on the left side of the stone chime knot (4–6), making sure both sides are identical. After completing the stone chime knot, make the loop of the necklace. Take four fine cords of two different colors and tie them together at irregular intervals with flat knots (8) (see *Chinese Knotting*, page 58). Make sure the knotted cords are long enough to go over the head. Tie both ends of the necklace loop into a button knot (9). Separate the four fine cord ends. Use two of the same color to embellish the rim of the stone chime knot, then hide the ends inside the knot body. Pull the other two same colored cords through the body of the stone chime knot and out the bottom. String the two cords with two glazed (or other) beads, then sew a button tassel (10) onto the end of them. Tie each tassel end into a cloverleaf knot (11) with two outer loops and bind them with gold thread.

135 For this charming ornament (see photograph page 24), fold a cord and tie three double connection knots (1–3) followed by an inverted butterfly knot (4) in which the *pan chang* knot that makes up the butterfly body is replaced with a round brocade knot. Make the two small wings from double coin knots. Then tie a five happiness knot (8). Extend each of the double coin knots on the outer rim into a butterfly knot (5, 6, 7, 9) identical to butterfly knot 4 above. After completing the five happiness knot, hide the cord ends inside the knot body of butterfly 9. Fold another cord and tie a stone chime knot (12). Tie its top right second and fourth side loops into a double coin knot (10). Hook up its bottom right corner loop with butterfly knot 9. Repeat the steps on the right (11), making sure the left and right sides are identical. After completing the stone chime knot, pull both cord ends up through the knot body and out through the top and tie a button tassel (13). Cut short two of the six tassel cords. Tie them into a double connection knot (14, 15) and bind the ends with gold thread. Separate two of the remaining tassel cords and tie them into a double coin knot (16) and hook them up with double coin knots 14 and 15, as shown above. Separate the cord ends of 16 and tie each into a double coin knot (17, 18). Hook up the two double coin knots. Pull the last two tassel cords through double coin knots 14 and 15, as shown, and tie each into a double coin knot (19, 20), then hook them up with the adjacent double coin knots 17 and 18. Finally, lightly sew together all the adjacent butterfly wings and secure the cord ends with strong glue.